Mrs. Troyer
14058 Cr. 28
Goshen, IN 46528

Index Map

ARCTIC OCEAN

Canada
pp. 30-31

Western and Cent
Europe
pp. 54-55

United States
pp. 32-33

ATLANTIC

Tropic of Cancer

Mexico, Central America,
and the Caribbean
pp. 34-35

PACIFIC

Equator

Northern South America
pp. 42-43

OCEAN

OCEAN

Tropic of Capricorn

Southern
South America
pp. 44-45

Antarctic Circle

Weddell
Sea

Legend

Drainage Symbols

Rhine **River**

Lake Baikal **Fresh lake**

Salt lake

Seasonal lake

Physical Features

Features such as mountains and deserts
are indicated by certain styles of type.

△ *Mt. Kosciusko*
7,310 Ft. **Mountain peak/elevation**

ROCKY MOUNTAINS
Rocky Mountains **Mountain range**

SAHARA
Sahara **Physical region**

Cape Horn **Cape**

KANGAROO ISLAND **Island**

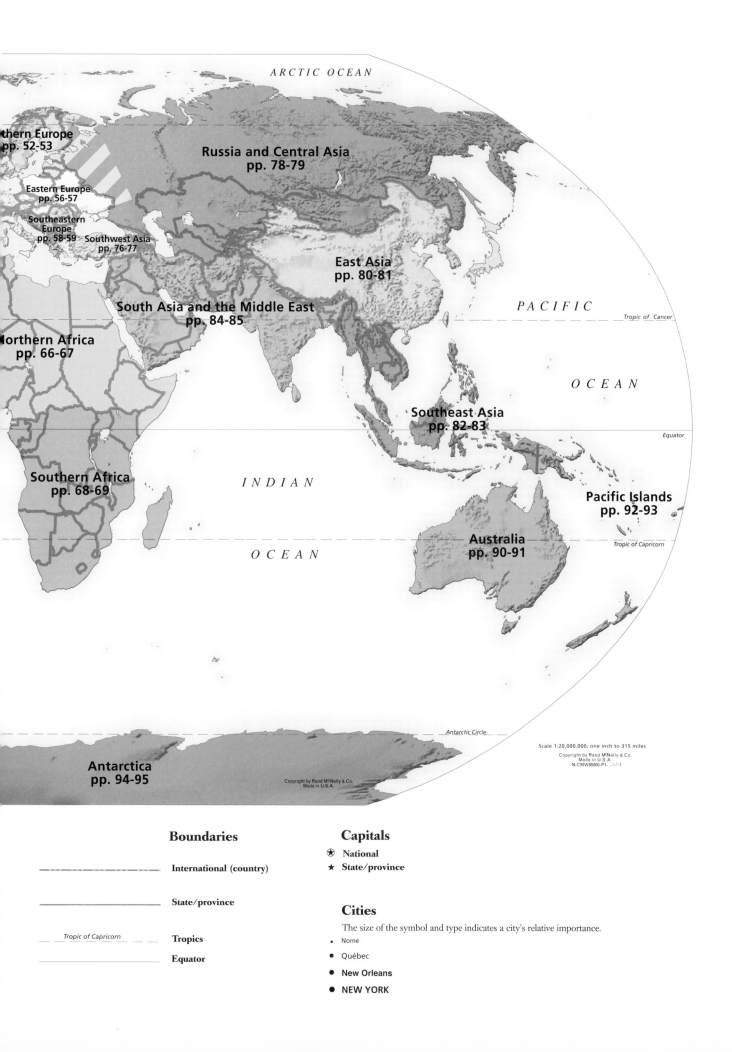

ARCTIC OCEAN

thern Europe
pp. 52-53

Russia and Central Asia
pp. 78-79

Eastern Europe
pp. 56-57

Southeastern
Europe
pp. 58-59   Southwest Asia
pp. 76-77

East Asia
pp. 80-81

PACIFIC

South Asia and the Middle East
pp. 84-85

Tropic of Cancer

Northern Africa
pp. 66-67

OCEAN

Southeast Asia
pp. 82-83

Equator

Southern Africa
pp. 68-69

INDIAN

Pacific Islands
pp. 92-93

Australia
pp. 90-91

Tropic of Capricorn

OCEAN

Antarctic Circle

Scale 1:20,000,000; one inch to 315 miles

Copyright by Rand McNally & Co.
Made in U.S.A.
N-CMW95000-P1- -1-1-1

Antarctica
pp. 94-95

Copyright by Rand McNally & Co.
Made in U.S.A.

Boundaries

——————————— International (country)

———————— State/province

Tropic of Capricorn Tropics

———————— Equator

Capitals

✪ National

★ State/province

Cities

The size of the symbol and type indicates a city's relative importance.

· Nome

● Québec

● **New Orleans**

● **NEW YORK**

President and CEO, Rand McNally & Company
Richard J. Davis

Senior Vice President, Marketing
Margaret A. Stender

Director, Reference and Children's Publishing
Kendra Ensor

Editors
Brett Gover
Chris Jaeggi
Bobby Mort
Ann Natunewicz
Nathalie Strassheim

Art Direction and Design
John Nelson
Donna McGrath

Writers
Leslie Morrison
Catherine VanPatten

Marketing
Leslie Hoadley
Alexsandra Sukhoy

Photo Research
Feldman & Associates, Inc.

Manufacturing
Terry D. Rieger

Cartography
Robert K. Argersinger
Gregory P. Babiak
Barbara Benstead-Strassheim
Marzee Eckhoff
Winifred V. Farbman
Robert Ferry
Amy Sayers
Nathan Schroeder
David Simmons
Jill M. Stift
Thomas Vitacco

RAND M℃NALLY

Children's Millennium® Atlas of the World
Copyright © 2000 by Rand McNally & Company

`randmcnally.com`   `randmcnallykids.com`

Published and printed in the United States of America

"Millennium" is a registered trademark of Rand McNally & Company
Rand McNally and Company.

   Children's millennium atlas of the World/Rand McNally.
   p. ; cm.
   At head of title: Rand McNally.
   Includes index.
   SUMMARY: Maps, photographs, illustrations, and text present information about the countries of the world, arranged by continents.
   ISBN 0-528-84205-6 (hardcover)
   ISBN 0-528-84207-2 (pbk.)
United States--Maps for children. 2. Children's atlases.
   1. Children's Atlases {1.Atlases. 2. Geography.] I. Title. II.
Title: Rand McNally children's millennium atlas of the world
   G1021 .R1647 1999 <G&M>
   912--dc21

99-16119
CIP
MAPS

For information on licensing and copyright permissions, please contact us at licensing@randmcnally.com

10 9 8 7 6 5 4 3 2 1

Photo Credits

(l = left, c = center, r = right, t = top, b = bottom)

© Mary Altier, 72 (b l)

Animals Animals:
© Dani/Jeske, 68 (b c)

Peter Arnold, Inc.:
© Fred Bavendam, 92 (b c); © Kevin Schafer, 46 (t); © Still Pictures/Mark Edwards, 16 (c l), 49 (t r); © Fritz Polking, 7 (t r), 68 (t l); © Bruno P. Zehnder, 90 (b r)

Black Star:
© F. Charton, 74 (b l)

© Cameramann International, Ltd., 80 (b c)

Bruce Coleman, Inc.:
© Andris Apse, 89 (c l); © Bruce Stewart, 88 (c l)

© Corbis/ *.Heaton*: 64 (b l)

Leo DeWyes, Inc.:
© DeWyes/D&J Heaton, 60 (t)

© European Space Agency, 6 (c)

FPG:
© Walter Bibikow, 31 (c r); © John Giustina, 15 (t r), 37 (b r), 81 (c r), 94-95 (b); © Mark Green, 26 (c l); © Peter Gridley, 24 (b l); © Steve Hix, 59 (b r); © G. Marche, 76 (c r); © Richard Price, 26 (c r); © Gail Shumway, 35 (b c); © Telegraph Colour Library, 70 (t), 80 (t l), 94 (t); © VCG, 15 (b r)

First Image West:
© Jim P. Garrison, 33 (b r)

© David R. Frazier Photolibrary, 49 (b l)

© Robert Fried Photography, 54 (b l)

H. Armstrong Roberts:
© B. Pogue, 56 (b l); © M. Schneider, 58 (b c); © Smith/Zefa, 88 (c r)

© Dave G. Houser, 91 (c r)

© Randall Hyman, 56 (c l)

© Jason Laure':
63 (c l); 64 (t r & b c)

Liaison International:
© Rob Johns, 27 (b l)

(c) Buddy Mays/TravelStock:
54 (t l), 88 (b), 91 (t)

© North Wind Picture Archives: 8 (Leif Ericsson, corn, iron plough), 9 (cotton gin, Abraham Lincoln, James Cook)

Odyssey Productions:
© Robert Frerck, 83 (c r)

Panoramic Images:
© China Photo Library, 70 (b); © Philip Gray, 86-87 (b); © Allen Prier, 24-25 (b); © K. Yamashita, 46 (b)

© Chip & Rosa Marie Peterson, 40 (b); 44 (c l)

© PhotoDisc, 8 (teacup), 11 (b r), 13 (b r), 33 (t r), 46 (b l), 60 (b l), 63 (b), 76 (b)

PhotoEdit:
© David Young-Wolff, 28 (b l)

Photo Researchers, Inc.:
© Tom McHugh, 89 (b l)

Photri:
77 (c l & c), 79 (cotton), 85 (Bangladesh); © Richard T. Nowitz, 74 (Muslims); © Fritz Prenzel Photo, 90 (b)

Reuters/Archive Photos: © Yannis Behrakis, 58 (t r)

© Eugene Schultz, 69 (b c)

© The Stock Market:
41 (b r); © David Ball, 6 (b l), 55 (c r); © Peter Beck, 27 (b r); © Tom Brakefield, 79 (b r); © Tibor Bognar, 85 (b r); © Alex Cabral, 43 (b r); © Murilo Dutra, 40 (t r); © Mark Ferri, 23 (b r), 50 (b l); © H.P. Merten, 53 (t r); © James Marshall, 43 (t c);

© M. Mastrorillo, 45 (b r); © J. Pollerross, 84 (b r); © Alan Reininger, 83 (t c); © Torleif Svensson, 83 (c), 85 (Indian man); © Ben Simmons, 49 (b r)

© Stock Montage, 10 (Atlas)

Tony Stone Images:
92 (c r), 95 (t r); © Jerry Alexander, 56 (b r); © Glen Allison, 33 (horse farm), 92 (t r); © Christopher Arnesen, 59 (t r); © Horst Baender, 31 (t r); © Alejandro Balaguer, 40 (c r); © James Balog, 28 (Inuit), 68 (b r); © David Barnes, 89 (c r); © John Beatty, 23 (t r); © Tom Bean, 34 (c l); © Oliver Benn, 28 (t r), 57 (t l); © Grilly Bernard, 66 (b l); © Randa Bishop, 39 (c r); © Gary Braasch, 14 (c l); © Ernest Braun, 21 (t r), 39 (b l); © Gary Brettnacher, 79 (b l); © Paula Bronstein, 59 (b l); © Bushnell/Soifer, 83 (t l); © Marc Chamberlain, 68 (c l); © Paul Chesley, 81 (b l), 82 (b l); © Connie Coleman, 6 (b r), 53 (t l); © Bruno De Hogues, 7 (t l), 64 (c l); © Nicholas DeVore, 53 (b c); © Florence Douyrou, 6 (b c), 50 (t l); © Wayne Eastep, 73 (t r); © Chad Ehlers, 92 (b l); © R. Elliot, 85 (t c); © Fred Felleman, 95 (b r); © Robert Frerck, 40 (t c); © Stephen Frink, 20 (b l), 89 (b r); © Louis Grandadam, 77 (b r); © Sylvain Grandadam, 7 (t r), 64 (b r), 84 (t l); © Bob Handelman, 28 (b l); © George Haling, 6 (c r), 44 (b r); © Elizabeth Harris, 6 (c l), 22 (b l), 40 (b r); © Mark Harris, 28 (playground); © Paul Harris, 7 (c r), 74 (t r); © Gary Hayes, 50 (c l); © William J. Hebert, 45 (c l); © David Hiser, 6 (c r), 33 (t l), 55 (t r); © Jeremy Horner, 9, 36 (t); © George Hunter, 83 (b r); © Warren Jacobs, 17 (t r), 63 (t r); © Jacques Jangoux, 43 (t l & t r); © Gavriel Jecan, 58 (c l), 59 (t l); © Darrell Jones, 16 (t l); © Richard Kavlin, 33 (surfers); © Paul Kenward, 44 (t l); © Jerry Kobalenko, 78 (b r); © John Lamb, 69 (b r); © Susan Lapides, 28 (waiters); © Jane Lewis, 84 (c l); © Mark Lewis, 35 (c r); © Renee Lynn, 64 (Masai); © Yves Marcoux, 30 (t c); © Sally Mayman, 66 (b r); © Steve Outram, 51 (b r); © Bryan Parsley, 21 (b r); © Richard Pasmore, 49 (c r); © Orion Press, 81 (t r); © Colin Pryor, 36-37 (b); © Kevin Schafer, 40 (t l), 79 (railway), 95 (c l); © Herb Schmitz, 76 (c l); © Ian Shaw, 56 (t r); © Hugh Sitton, 69 (t r); © Charles Sleicher, 34 (b r); © Philip & Karen Smith; 44 (b l); © Robin Smith, 90 (b l); © Sarah Stone, 35 (t r); © James Strachan, 66 (b c), 79 (t r); © Keren Su, 72 (t r); © T. Resource, 44 (t r); © Tom Till, 6 (c l), 17 (b r), 24 (t); © Traveler's Resource, 73 (b l); © P. Tweedie, 90 (t); © Marie Ueda, 7 (kangaroo); © Larry Ulrich, 32 (b l); © Steve Vidler, 57 (t r), 63 (c r); © Rosemary Weller, 63 (c l); © Randy Wells, 35 (b r); © Art Wolfe, 19 (t r), 55 (b r), 68 (b l)

© SuperStock:
6 (Galileo), 7 (c l & fan), 8 (Christopher Columbus, Normans, Medici, Gutenberg, Arab traders, Ming mask), 9 (Model T, Galileo, Isaac Newton), 18 (b l), 19 (b r), 28 (b r), 30 (c l, b l, and b c), 38 (t r), 39 (t r), 42 (b l), 48 (c l), 52 (b r), 64 (t l and c r), 70 (c l), 74 (c l, c, and monks), 75 (c r), 80 (b r), 81 (b r), 82 (c l), 86 (t); © Avid Northcott, 43 (c r)

Vandystadt/Allsport
© Jean-Marc Loubat, 55 (b l)

Viesti:
© M. Downey, 75 (t r)

Visuals Unlimited:
© Bill Kamin, 58 (b r); © Steve McCutcheon, 9, 62 (t l)

© Randy Wells, 50 (b c)

RAND M:NALLY

Children's

Millennium® Atlas of the World

Contents

World Front Section

North America

South America

Europe

Millennium Timeline (The Years 1000-2000 A.D.)

	1000-1100	1100-1200	1200-1300	1300-1400	1400-1500	
North America	c. **1000** Leif Ericsson and the Vikings sail to North America. c. **1100** Anasazi begin building Mesa Verde cliff dwelling in southwestern North America.	**1100-1200** Hohokam of Arizona begin to build platform temple mounds for worship.	c. **1200** Thousands live in and around Cahokia, a city of temple mounds built by the Mississippians. **1275-1300** Severe drought in Chaco Canyon hastens collapse of Anasazi communities.	**1300s** Warrior knights help make Aztecs a powerful society in Mexico. **1325** Aztecs found city of Tenochtitlán, now Mexico City.	**1492** Christopher Columbus lands in the Caribbean, but thinks he is in the East Indies.	
South America	c. **1000** Peruvian farmers grow potatoes and corn for food.	**1100s** Incas in Peru make sculptures of their warrior chiefs.	c. **1250** Mayan culture becomes stronger, and a new capital city is built. c. **1250** Chimu people along northern coast of Peru expand their empire.	c.**1300s** Inca people in Peru become skilled builders. Inca culture expands into the central Andes region.	**1400s** Inca empire covers most of the west coast of South America. c. **1450** Incas build Machu Picchu in Peru. **1470s** Chimu culture in Northern Peru collapses.	
Europe	c. **1050** Iron plows replace wooden plows in Europe. **1066** Norman conquest of England.	**1119** First European University established in Bologna, Italy. **1124-1153** David I rules Scotland. **1152-1190** Frederick I rules powerful Holy Roman Empire.	**1215** King John of England signs the Magna Carta, limiting royal power. **1233** Coal is mined in Newcastle, England, for the first time. **1298** English archers use longbows to defeat Scottish army.	**1378-1381** Workers' Revolt in Florence, Italy (1378) and Peasants' Revolt in England (1381). **1397** Medici family establish themselves as bankers in Florence.	**1440s** Nicolas Cusanus claims the Earth is in constant motion and that space is infinite. c. **1450** Johannes Gutenberg invents the printing press.	
Africa	**1000s** Bantu-speaking people hunt and farm in Africa. **1000s** West African kingdoms flourish from gold trade in Africa.	c. **1100** Empire of Ghana begins to decline. c. **1100** Arab traders settle in Africa along Indian Ocean coast. **1173** Muslim warrior Saladin declares himself sultan of Egypt.	**1200s** The town of Great Zimbabwe is built by the Shona people in southern Africa. c. **1235** Mali empire in West Africa becomes more powerful.	**1348** The Black Plague devastates Egyptian population. c. **1350** Great Zimbabwe in southern Africa flourishes in gold trade. **1380** Kongo kingdom begins in the Congo River region of Zaire.	c. **1420** Portuguese sailors explore west coast of Africa. **1468** Sanghai Empire dominates central Sudan in Africa.	
Asia	c. **1000** Indian mathematician Sridhara recognizes the importance of zero. c. **1000** Chinese begin to use gunpowder for warfare. **1041** Chinese printer Pi Sheng invents moveable type.	c. **1100** Chinese explain the causes of solar and lunar eclipses. **1100s** Sultan of Baghdad probably the first to use pigeons for mail system. **1191** Tea arrives in Japan from China.	**1206** Genghis Khan unites the Mongols. **1232** Chinese build first rockets, which resembled fireworks. **1259-1260** Important astronomical observatories are built in Maragha, Iran, and Beijing, China.	c. **1300** Ottoman dynasty begins in Turkey. **1368** Ming dynasty begins in China. c. **1390** Ottoman Turks conquer Asia Minor.	**1419-1450** Korea prospers under King Sejong. **1448-1488** Thailand expands under King Trailok. c. **1498** Portuguese sailor Vasco de Gama reaches India.	
Australia and Oceania	c. **1000** Maoris settle in present-day New Zealand, where they hunt and gather.	**1100s** Polynesians establish settlements on the island of Pitcairn.	c. **1200** On Tonga, Tui Tonga monarchy builds coral platform for worship.	**1350** Maoris prosper on New Zealand's North Island.	c. **1400** Tonga people build a ceremonial center at Mu'a in the South Pacific.	

1500-1600	1600-1700	1700-1800	1800-1900	1900-2000
1500s Europeans explore North America and claim land for their countries. **1519-1521** Hernando Cortés of Spain conquers the Aztecs. **1534** French explorer Jacques Cartier travels to Canada. **1540s** Spanish come to California.	**1607** English establish first permanent colony in North America at Jamestown, Virginia. **1608** Québec founded by French settlers. **1619** First African slaves brought to North America. **1625** Dutch found New Amsterdam (later called New York).	**1775** American Revolution begins. **1776** Declaration of Independence approved. **1792** New York Stock Exchange is organized. **1793** Eli Whitney invents cotton gin. **1796** Edward Jenner develops smallpox vaccine.	**1804** Lewis and Clark begin exploring route to Pacific Ocean. **1861-1865** U.S. Civil War. **1863** Lincoln issues the Emancipation Proclamation. **1876** Alexander Graham Bell invents the telephone.	**1908** Ford Motor Company produces first Model "T" automobile. **1960s** Martin Luther King, Jr. leads civil rights protests in U.S. **1969** Moon landing. **1979** Sandinistas take control of Nicaragua. **1990** Launch of Hubble Space Telescope.
1533 Francisco Pizarro of Spain conquers the Inca empire in South America.	**1608** Jesuits establish state of Paraguay. **1654** Portuguese drive Dutch from Brazil.	**1726** Spanish found city of Montevideo in Uruguay. **1727** Coffee first planted in Brazil. **1742** Native Americans of Peru rebel against Spaniards. **1763** Rio de Janeiro becomes Brazil's capital.	**1810** Simón Bolívar emerges to lead Latin American revolutions. **1825** Bolívar founds state of Bolivia. **1828** Uruguay becomes independent. **1879-1884** Chile, Peru, Bolivia at war. **1891** Civil war in Chile.	**1955** Military officials seize power from Argentinian president Peron. **1982** Falklands war between Argentina and Britain.
1506-1507 First maps of the New World are printed in Europe. **1519** Ferdinand Magellan sets sail from Spain to circumnavigate the globe. **1514-1565** Explorers introduce pineapples, coffee, chocolate, sweet potatoes, corn, and tobacco to Europe.	**1608** Galileo makes astronomical observations using newly invented telescope. **1628** William Harvey describes the circulation of blood in the body. **1687** Isaac Newton describes the fundamental laws of motion.	**1715** Daniel Fahrenheit develops first mercury thermometer. **1742** Anders Celsius creates thermometer marking 0° as freezing and 100° as boiling. **1789** French Revolution begins.	**1804** Napoleon becomes emperor of the French. **1859** Charles Darwin publishes book about the evolution of species. **1884** Greenwich, England established as the zero meridian for time zones. **1896** Italian Marconi invents wireless telegraph.	**1914-1918** World War I. **1916** Albert Einstein publishes his General Theory of Relativity. **1928** Alexander Fleming discovers penicillin. **1939-1945** World War II. **1989** Berlin Wall, built in 1961, is torn down. **1990** East and West Germany are united.
1530s Slave trade begins, organized by the Portuguese. **1562** African slaves are sent to the Americas as the English slave trade begins.	**c. 1650** Ethiopia expels Portuguese missionaries and diplomats. **1652** Dutch establish Cape Town in South Africa. **1680s** Asante kingdom rises in West Africa. **1686** Louis XIV of France annexes Madagascar.	**c. 1710** The 300-year-old African Kingdom of Kongo collapses after Portuguese invasion. **1724-1734** African leaders stop slave trade in West Africa. **1740s** Slave trade resumes. **1755** Sailors bring first outbreak of smallpox to Cape Town.	**1822** Liberia founded as home for freed U.S. slaves. **1830** French invade Algeria. **1873-1874** Asante and British at war. **1879** Zulu and British at war. **1880s** Nearly all of Africa is colonized by European countries.	**1931** Railway from Angola to Mozambique completed. **1963** Organization of African Unity founded. **1980** Zimbabwe is the last African country to gain independence from colonial rule. **1990** Nelson Mandela elected president of South Africa.
1520-1566 Ottoman Empire at its peak. **1526** Mongols invade India, establishing Mogul Empire. **1533** Ivan the Terrible rules as the first tsar of Russia.	**1630s** Japan expels most foreigners, allowing trade only with the Dutch and Chinese. **1644** Manchus invade China, establish the Quing dynasty.	**1735-1795** Chinese empire reaches its furthest extent. **1763** Britain becomes dominant power in India. **1783-1788** Japan experiences severe famine. **1784** U.S. begins trade with China.	**1804** Russia attempts but fails to establish trade with Japan. **1854** U.S. opens Japan to trade. **1857** Native soldiers in India rebel against English rulers. **1872** First Japanese railway opens.	**1900** Boxer Rebellion in China. **1917** Bolshevik Revolution in Russia. **1920** In India, Gandhi leads a peaceful non-cooperation movement. **1939-1945** World War II. **1957** Russians launch Sputnik space satellite. **1965-1973** Vietnam War.
1526 Portuguese land on Papua New Guinea. **1550s** Maoris in New Zealand build fortified enclosures.	**1600s** Dutch sailors discover the north and west coasts of Australia by accident. **1642-1644** Abel Tasman explores Tasmania and New Zealand.	**1768-1771** British Captain James Cook's first voyage to the Pacific. **1788** British begin to settle Australia with prisoners, creating a penal colony.	**1801-1803** Matthew Flinders circumnavigates and names Australia. **1851** Gold found in southeastern Australia.	**1901** British colonies become states, form the Commonwealth of Australia. **1933** Australia takes control of a large part of Antarctica. **2000** Sydney, Australia the site of the Summer Olympic Games.

The Basics of Maps and Cartography

What is a Map?

A map is a picture—or representation—of a place. Most maps are drawn to show places from above. When you think of maps, you might picture a folded road map or a wall map that hangs in the classroom. But, there are many different kinds of maps. Satellite images, or pictures of Earth taken from space, are maps. Floor plans of houses are maps too, because they show where each room is. In fact, you probably keep a lot of maps in your head. These "mental" maps help you remember how to get to school or your friend's house without needing to ask directions every time.

This satellite image of the San Francisco Bay area clearly shows the shape of the coastline.

On this road map of San Francisco, you can get information on street names and points of interest.

An atlas is a book of maps. In 1570, Abraham Ortelius developed the first modern atlas, although he didn't call it by that name. Another man, Gerardus Mercator, first used the term "atlas" in 1589 when he named his collection of maps after a person from mythology named Atlas. In Greek mythology, Atlas was forced to support the world on his shoulders as punishment for warring against the gods. Although the word "atlas" is still used to mean a book of maps, atlases today may contain diagrams, tables, and text, in addition to maps.

Atlas

People who make maps are called "mapmakers" or "cartographers." Cartography is the art of making maps. The word comes from the Latin **carta**, meaning "map" and the Greek **graph** meaning "write."

History of Mapmaking

Thousands of years ago, ancient people developed the first maps as they explored new places and settled new lands. The Chinese, the Arabs, and the Indians were among the first people to experiment with mapmaking, creating maps by drawing on animal skins and rocks, and by carving maps on stones and in wood. In Babylon, an ancient Middle Eastern civilization, people carved maps into stone tablets. Ancient Egyptians drew maps on papyrus (a plant made into paper) and carved them into temple walls. Several thousand years ago, Europeans drew maps on paper, using the maps to help find their way across oceans to new lands and then to guide them home safely.

Ancient Greeks made and used globes, which are three-dimensional models of Earth. The Greeks divided the globe into segments, using lines of latitude and longitude. Later, these lines were overlaid onto flat maps. Today we still use latitude and longitude to find places on globes and maps.

Lines of latitude and longitude intersect on a globe to form a grid.

This map, drawn in 1587, shows what North and South America were thought to look like at the time.

AMERICAE SIVE NOVI ORBIS, NOVA DESCRIPTIO.

Major Types of Maps

Political Maps

Many of the maps you see are political maps. Political maps show how people have divided up the land on Earth. Using different colors, political maps show the borders between countries, states, provinces, and territories. The maps also show the location of cities, which are represented by different size type to indicate populations, roads, parks, and other features.

Physical Maps

Physical maps use different colors to show the elevation, or height, of land and the depth of water on the surface of the earth. Physical maps help readers see mountains, valleys, oceans, lakes, and rivers. Each physical map has its own legend, which explains which colors represent various elevations of land and depths of water.

Thematic Maps

Thematic maps use different colors to give information about specific themes or topics, such as populations, climates, languages spoken, or economies in different parts of the world. You can use thematic maps to compare and contrast information on one map or between several maps. Like physical maps, each thematic map has its own legend.

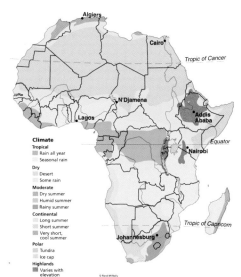

Locator Maps

Locator maps are small, simple maps that show what continent, region, or state is featured on a more detailed map. Locators point out where the maps are in relation to a larger area.

Maps Today

During the past 50 years, mapping around the world has become very precise. Sophisticated computers use information taken from satellite images–photos of Earth taken from space–and other sources to produce highly accurate maps used by people in business, government, and education. Students use maps to learn about foreign countries. Business people use maps to decide where to sell new products. And governmental agencies, like local fire and police departments, use maps to pinpoint houses and their residents who may need assistance.

Maps are available in a variety of places and formats. In addition to reading paper maps, you can use maps on your computer–with special mapping software or on the Internet. If you'd like to see and use a special set of Rand McNally digital maps–for homework or just for fun–you can access our special kids' Web site at:

randmcnallykids.com

How to Use This Atlas

By definition, an atlas is a book of maps. Therefore, to use an atlas you need to understand a few things about reading maps. The sections below explain how to use the maps in this atlas, as well as other parts of the book.

Finding Places

Finding places in an atlas is an adventure–a journey that takes you across rivers, over mountains, and into new countries. To find places in the Rand McNally's *Children's Millennium® Atlas of the World*, use the following tools:

Index Map

At the very front of the book is an index map. The index map shows each of the seven continents in a different color, and it lists the pages where you'll find the maps for each continent.

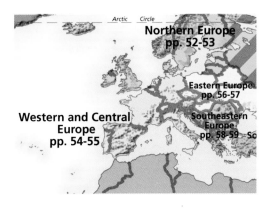

Index

At the very back of the book is the index–a list of the many places (such as cities, towns, and countries) and features (such as mountains and rivers) shown on the maps. The index tells you the page where you'll find each place or feature, and it also includes a letter-and-number code that tells you exactly where to look on the map to find the place or feature.

Map Grids

To help you locate places and features, each map includes a "map grid" along its four sides. Along the left and right sides are letters, and along the top and bottom sides are numbers. The letter-and-number codes in the index correspond to the letters and numbers along the sides of the maps.

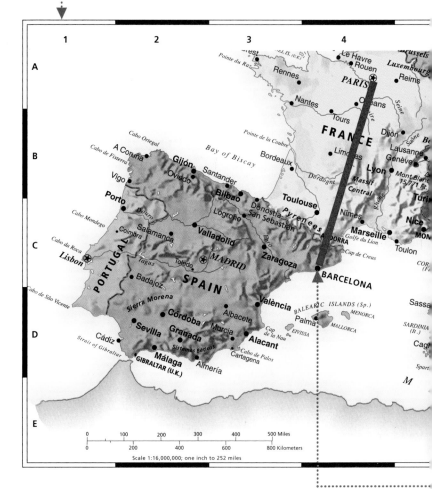

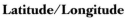

Latitude/Longitude

Imaginary lines that run vertically from the top of the earth to the bottom are called lines of longitude. These lines, which meet at the top of the earth and at the bottom, are also called meridians. The imaginary lines that run horizontally around the globe are called lines of latitude. These lines, which are parallel to one another and therefore never meet, are also known as parallels. The equator, which runs around the very middle of the earth, is the best known line of latitude.

These imaginary lines of longitude and latitude cross and form grids, which help you find places on a map or globe. In this atlas, the equator, the Tropic of Cancer, and the Tropic of Capricorn– all lines of latitude–are shown.

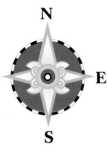

Knowing Direction

Each of the maps in this atlas includes something called a compass rose–a circle with arrows and the letters N, S, E, and W. These letters represent the four main points of a compass: North, South, East, and West. (On some old maps, the compass roses are beautifully illustrated and include so many direction points that they actually look like flowering roses!)

This is an example of an ornate compass rose.

Using the Legend

Maps contain all sorts of information. The legend, sometimes called the "map key," explains the symbols that appear on the maps. Symbols are icons that represent something else. For example, a black star in a circle is the symbol for a capital city. So in France, you'll find a ✷ next to Paris, the capital city. Other symbols on the maps represent rivers, lakes, mountain peaks, and borders between countries.

The main legend in this atlas is located below the index map in the very front of the book. The physical maps and thematic maps all have legends next to them, on the same page.

River   Fresh Lake   Salt Lake   Seasonal Lake

Understanding Terms

This atlas includes a glossary on page 104. In the glossary you will find explanations of many geographic terms used in the atlas.

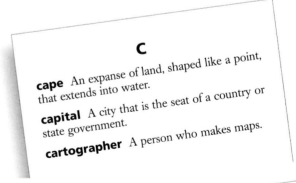

C

cape An expanse of land, shaped like a point, that extends into water.

capital A city that is the seat of a country or state government.

cartographer A person who makes maps.

Measuring Distance

Next to every map is a scale bar that shows how the size of the map relates to the real world. The scale bar also allows you to measure the distance between places. For example, let's say that one inch on a map scale represents about 250 miles in the real world, and that, using a ruler, you measured 2 inches between the cities of Paris, France, and Barcelona, Spain. Since one inch equals about 250 miles, then 2 inches must equal about 500 miles. This means that the distance between Paris and Barcelona in the real world is approximately 500 miles. Instead of using a ruler to measure distances, you can mark points along the edge of a piece of paper and then use the scale bar to measure the distance between the points.

| 0 | 100 | 200 | 300 | 400 | 500 Miles |

| 0 | 200 | 400 | 600 | 800 Kilometers |

Scale 1:16,000,000; one inch to 252 miles

Learning about Countries

If you want to learn some basic facts about any country, or to see what its flag looks like, turn to the Country Flag and Fact File that begins on page 96. This section shows each country's flag and lists its size, population, and capital city.

Togo
Area: 21,925 sq mi (56,785 sq km)
Population: 4,992,000
Capital: Lomé

World Climates

This map shows the climate zones of the world. Climate describes the weather conditions that occur in an area over a long period of time–not weeks and months, but years. The legend to the right of the map shows the specific climates that you can find on the map.

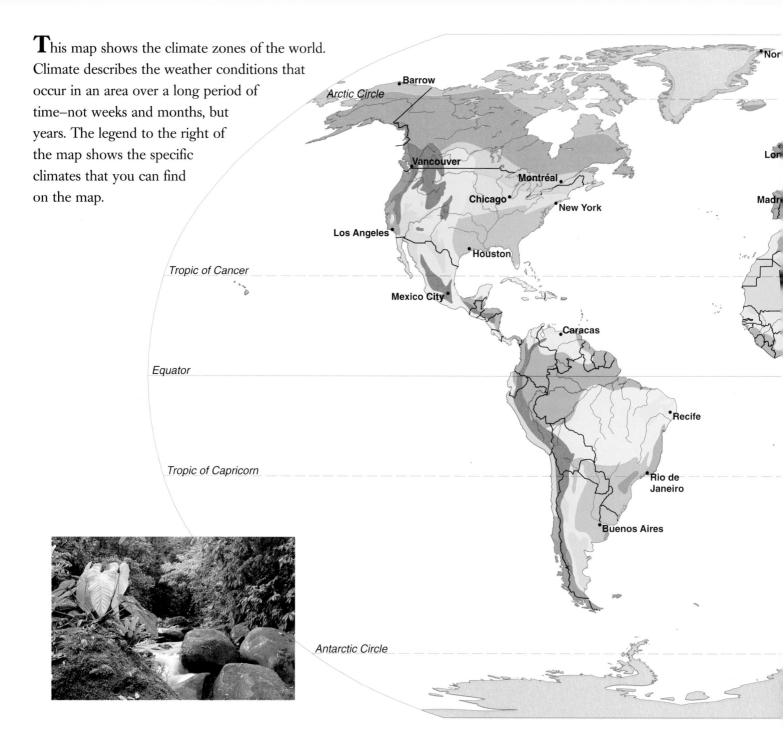

Climates are created by temperature and precipitation (rain, snow), and climates around the world vary for different reasons. In general, Earth's climates grow hotter as you approach the equator, and become colder as you move north or south from the equator. This is because the Sun's rays hit Earth most directly and most often in the tropics–the area between the Tropic of Cancer and the Tropic of Capricorn. Also, climates tend to be cooler in areas with high elevations because the thinner air high up holds less heat. Finally, areas that lie along the coast of an ocean or sea often have climates much milder than that of inland areas, thanks to ocean breezes and currents.

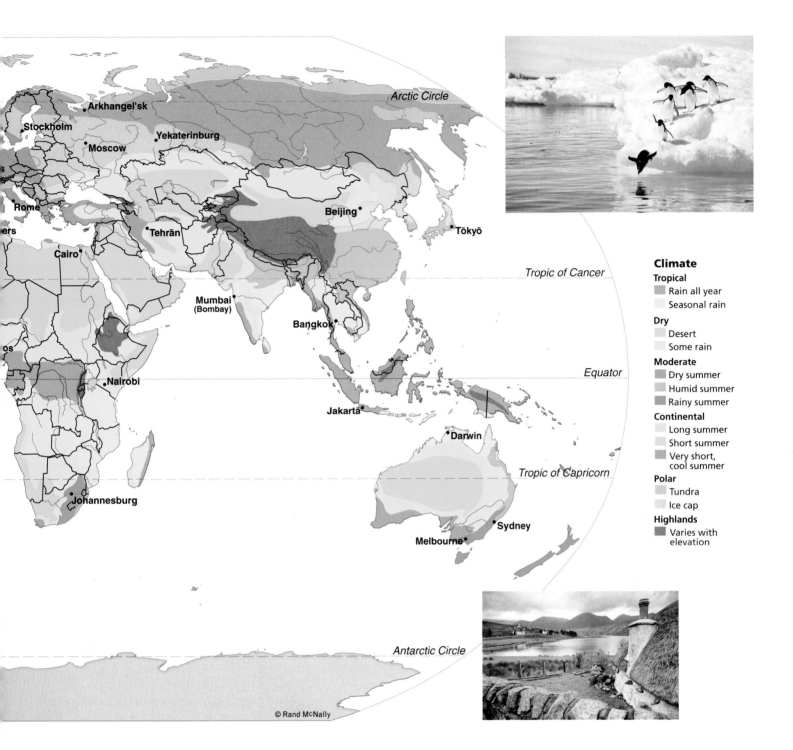

Climate

Tropical
- Rain all year
- Seasonal rain

Dry
- Desert
- Some rain

Moderate
- Dry summer
- Humid summer
- Rainy summer

Continental
- Long summer
- Short summer
- Very short, cool summer

Polar
- Tundra
- Ice cap

Highlands
- Varies with elevation

© Rand McNally

Precipitation is the other factor that determines climate. Usually, areas of heaviest precipitation are found along the equator, where warm tropical air holds the greatest amount of water vapor. The reddish colors on the map show areas that experience tropical climates: the great rain forests of northern South America, central Africa, and Indonesia.

The terrain, or physical features, of an area also affects precipitation. When the terrain blocks the flow of breezes, it can dramatically alter the pattern of rainfall. Tall mountain ranges force moist air currents to rise above them, and when the air descends on the other side of the mountain, it releases moisture in the form of heavy rains. This "rainshadow effect"–where one side of a mountain range receives abundant rainfall and the other is desert–can be observed in the northwestern United States and in Chile west and east of the Andes.

The climate we live in directly affects our lifestyles. The type of clothing we wear, the foods we eat, the way we travel, and the home we inhabit–all are dictated by climate.

World Economies

This map identifies economic activity around the world. The colors of the different areas on the map explain how most of the people in a particular area make their living.

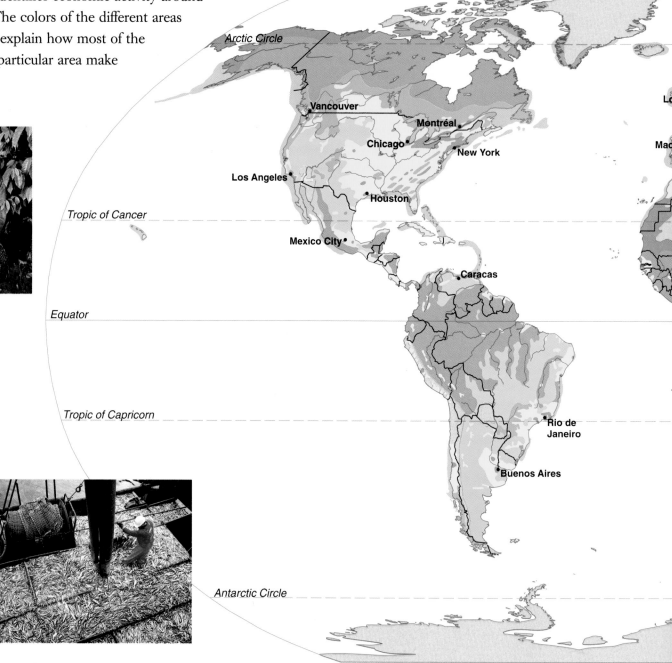

The physical characteristics of the land, such as fertile valleys and oil-rich plains, determine how people are able to use it and make livings. Compare this map to the World Physical map on pages 20-21. In general, areas where farming takes place (shown in yellow on this World Economies map) contain some of Earth's most fertile soils. Food harvested from the wide plains and river valleys of Europe, southeastern Asia, and central North America feeds much of the world's population. In some countries, such as India and China, agriculture is the major way to earn a living. In Brazil and the countries of eastern Europe, however, a much smaller part of the work force raises crops. This fraction is even smaller in Canada, the United States, and western Europe.

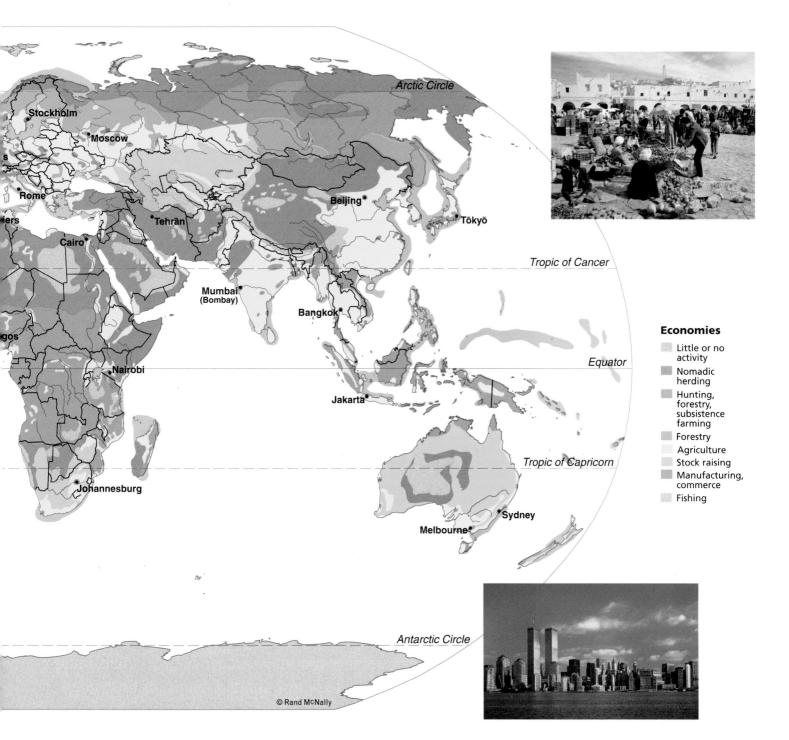

Arctic Circle

Stockholm

Moscow

Rome

Cairo

Tehrān

Beijing

Tōkyō

Tropic of Cancer

Mumbai
(Bombay)

Bangkok

Nairobi

Equator

Jakarta

Tropic of Capricorn

Johannesburg

Sydney

Melbourne

Antarctic Circle

© Rand McNally

Economies

- Little or no activity
- Nomadic herding
- Hunting, forestry, subsistence farming
- Forestry
- Agriculture
- Stock raising
- Manufacturing, commerce
- Fishing

Very few regions of the world are used for manufacturing and trade. These areas are sometimes called "developed." In the United States, for instance, developed areas grew near transportation routes and land that contained natural resources such as minerals. Major manufacturing centers such as Chicago and Montréal line the shores of the Great Lakes and the St. Lawrence Seaway, an important

transportation route that provides access to the Atlantic Ocean. Likewise, Germany's Ruhr Valley has long provided mineral resources, and the country's position in the center of Europe has helped it grow into a major industrial force.

In general, countries that are more economically developed have a greater range of industries than less developed countries. This is because people are able to specialize in the work that they do best, and use the money that they earn to pay for other goods and services that they need.

World Population

This map shows where people live in the world. The legend to the right of the map explains what the different colors mean in terms of population density. Population density is a measure of the number of people living in each square mile (2.59 square kilometers) of land.

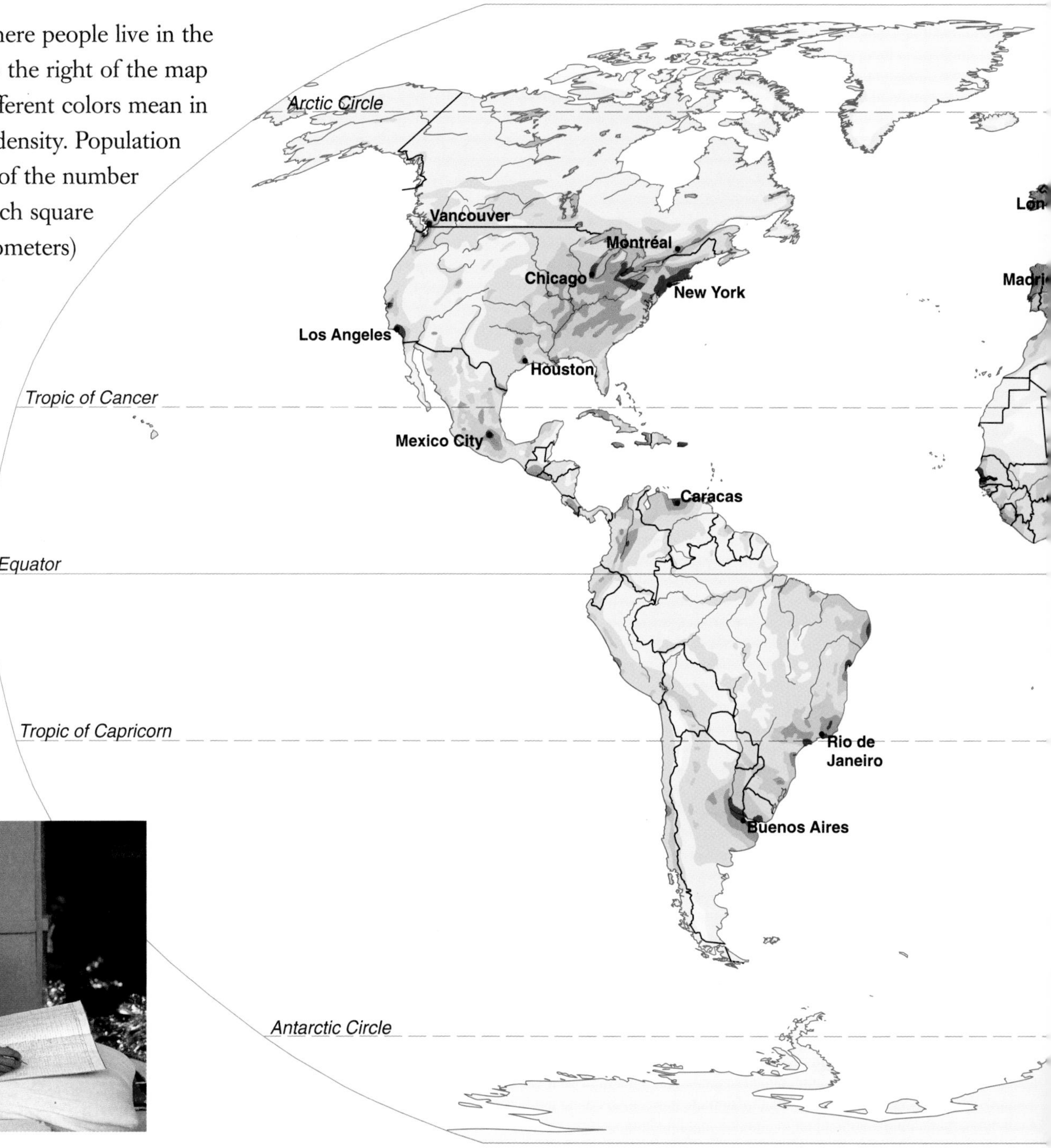

Arctic Circle

Vancouver

Montréal

Chicago

New York

Los Angeles

Houston

Tropic of Cancer

Mexico City

Caracas

Equator

Tropic of Capricorn

Rio de Janeiro

Buenos Aires

Antarctic Circle

Lon

Madri

Population densities vary for many reasons, including climate and terrain. For example, the continent of Antarctica–Earth's coldest region–is uninhabited, meaning that no one lives there permanently. Its harsh climate makes living there nearly impossible.

Lands with favorable climates and terrains tend to be densely populated, especially if they are good for farming. The presence of the Nile River explains the ribbon of dense population that runs through the desert lands of Sudan and Egypt in northern Africa: People live and farm close to its fertile banks. In the vast rain forests of South America, people settle along the Amazon River.

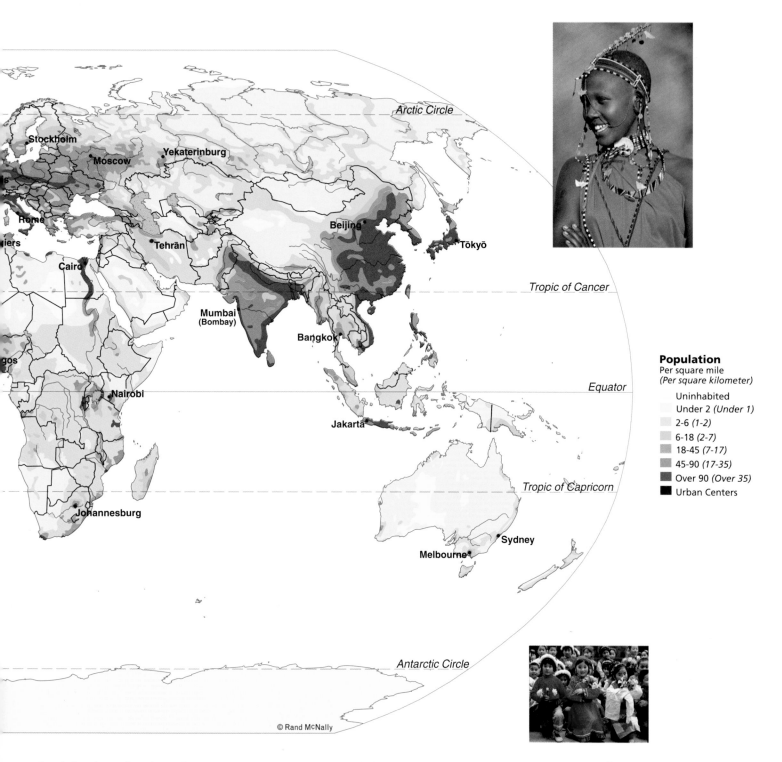

Stockholm
Moscow
Yekaterinburg
Rome
Tehrān
Cairo
Beijing
Tōkyō
Mumbai
(Bombay)
Bangkok
Nairobi
Jakarta
Johannesburg
Sydney
Melbourne

Arctic Circle
Tropic of Cancer
Equator
Tropic of Capricorn
Antarctic Circle

© Rand McNally

Population
Per square mile
(Per square kilometer)

Uninhabited
Under 2 *(Under 1)*
2-6 *(1-2)*
6-18 *(2-7)*
18-45 *(7-17)*
45-90 *(17-35)*
Over 90 *(Over 35)*
Urban Centers

Look for the red and purple regions—they represent the world's most densely populated areas. The huge populations of India and China are settled in Asia's rich farmlands. For the most part, most of these people still live away from cities in country, or rural, areas.

In Europe and the United States, by contrast, the most populous areas are cities, or urban areas, which grew up near farmland, resources, and trade routes, especially waterways. In the United States, people are concentrated along the Atlantic and Pacific Oceans, the shores of the Great Lakes, and the banks of the Mississippi River. Cities contain the majority of the population of Australia, Argentina, Canada, France, Japan, and the United States.

Japan is one of the world's most densely populated countries. Slightly smaller than the state of California, it holds more than 126 million people.

World Physical

This map shows the physical features found on the surface of the earth. The colors and shading on the map indicate the kind of terrain found in that area of the world. The legend to the right of the map explains what the colors mean.

ARCTIC OCEAN

GREENLAND

Baffin Bay

BAFFIN ISLAND

Arctic Circle

ICELAND

FAROE

BRITISH ISLES

Yukon

Mt. McKinley 20,320 ft.

Mackenzie

Canadian Shield

Hudson Bay

NEWFOUNDLAND

Rocky Mountains

NORTH AMERICA

Great Plain

St. Lawrence

Appalachian Mts.

Colorado

Mississippi

Cape Hatteras

AZORES

Iberian Peninsula

ALEUTIAN ISLANDS

ATLANTIC

CANARY ISLANDS

Atlas

PACIFIC

Tropic of Cancer

HAWAIIAN ISLANDS

Baja California

Gulf of Mexico

CUBA

HISPANIOLA

JAMAICA

Caribbean Sea

OCEAN

CAPE VERDE ISLANDS

Cap Vert

A

Niger

OCEAN

TRINIDAD

Orinoco

Equator

GALAPAGOS ISLANDS

Amazon

Amazon

Cabo de São Roque

Basin

SOUTH

SAMOA ISLANDS

Andes

Planalto do Mato Grosso

ST. HELENA

Tropic of Capricorn

AMERICA

Paraná

Cerro Aconcagua 22,831 ft.

0   400   800   1200 1600 2000 Miles
0   600   1200 1800 2400 3000 Kilometers
Scale 1:163,000,000; one inch to 2573 miles

Copyright by Rand McNally & Co.
Made in U.S.A.
N-CMW10000-A1- -1-1-1

Andes

Patagonia

FALKLAND IS.

SOUTH GEORGIA

Cape Horn

TIERRA DEL FUEGO

Antarctic Circle

Antarctic Peninsula

Weddell Sea

Ross Sea

Marie Byrd Land

Vinson Massif 16,066 ft.

A N

More than three-quarters of Earth is covered by water, including four large oceans and many smaller seas, all made up of salt water. Fresh water–water without salt–is most often found in smaller inland lakes and rivers, such as the Great Lakes in North America.

The remaining part of Earth's surface is made up of landmasses with mountains, deserts, rivers, lakes, and plateaus. The floors of oceans and seas also have mountains and valleys, but you can't see them because they're underwater. This map shows the names and different categories of Earth's physical features.

Earth's surface is called the crust, a wrinkled layer of solid rock that is constantly changing. The crust is cracked into a dozen separate fragments called "tectonic plates," which float on a sea of dense, semi-liquid rock far below the surface. Columns of this molten rock slowly rise and fall, nudging the bases of the crustal plates that float on Earth's surface. As the plates try to move, they push into neighboring plates.

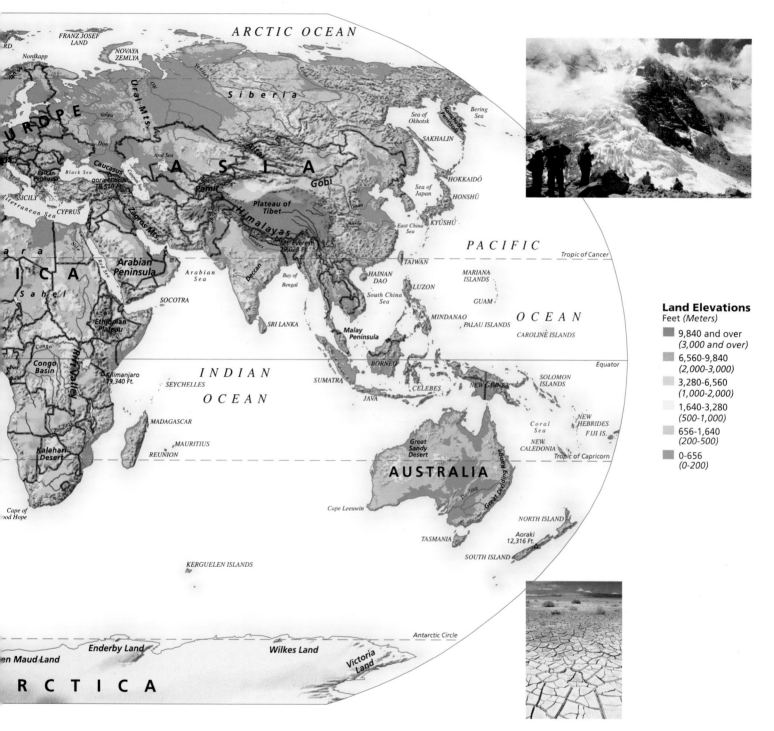

ARCTIC OCEAN

FRANZ JOSEF LAND

Nordkapp

NOVAYA ZEMLYA

Siberia

Ural Mts.

Ob

Yenisey

Lena

Kamchatka Peninsula

Bering Sea

Sea of Okhotsk

SAKHALIN

Volga

A S I A

Don

EUROPE

Caucasus

Black Sea

Caspian Sea

gora Elbrus 18,510 ft.

Pamir

Gobi

HOKKAIDŌ

Sea of Japan

HONSHŪ

Plateau of Tibet

Zagros Mts.

Balkan Peninsula

SICILY

CYPRUS

Mediterranean Sea

Himalayas

Amur

Huan

Yangtze

KYŪSHŪ

East China Sea

Mt. Everest 29,028 Ft.

Nile

Red Sea

ara

ICA

Sahel

Arabian Peninsula

Arabian Sea

SOCOTRA

Deccan

Bay of Bengal

Ganges

TAIWAN

HAINAN DAO

LUZON

South China Sea

MARIANA ISLANDS

PACIFIC

Tropic of Cancer

SRI LANKA

Malay Peninsula

MINDANAO

GUAM

PALAU ISLANDS

OCEAN

CAROLINE ISLANDS

Congo

Congo Basin

Rift Valley

Kilimanjaro 19,340 Ft.

INDIAN

SEYCHELLES

SUMATRA

JAVA

BORNEO

CELEBES

NEW GUINEA

SOLOMON ISLANDS

Equator

Zambezi

OCEAN

MADAGASCAR

Coral Sea

NEW HEBRIDES

FIJI IS.

Kalahari Desert

MAURITIUS

REUNION

Great Sandy Desert

NEW CALEDONIA

Tropic of Capricorn

AUSTRALIA

Great Dividing Range

Cape of Good Hope

Cape Leeuwin

Darling

NORTH ISLAND

Aoraki 12,316 Ft.

TASMANIA

SOUTH ISLAND

KERGUELEN ISLANDS

Antarctic Circle

en Maud Land

Enderby Land

Wilkes Land

Victoria Land

RCTICA

Land Elevations
Feet *(Meters)*

- 9,840 and over *(3,000 and over)*
- 6,560-9,840 *(2,000-3,000)*
- 3,280-6,560 *(1,000-2,000)*
- 1,640-3,280 *(500-1,000)*
- 656-1,640 *(200-500)*
- 0-656 *(0-200)*

Over millions of years, the pushing, grinding, and colliding of tectonic plates has crumpled, folded, and lifted rock, slowly building up the world's great mountain ranges. For instance, the Appalachian Mountains in eastern North America resulted from a collision between North America and Africa some 320 million years ago. Likewise,

the Himalayas–the highest mountains in the world–were forced upward when India rammed into Asia. On this map, you can see where Earth's mountains have formed.

The map also shows the world's desert regions. Deserts are dry lands with low rainfall and sparse plant and animal life. Not all deserts are hot, sandy, and sunny. They can also be cold, rocky, or ice-covered.

World Political

This map shows the countries of the world. Unlike the other maps in this section, the map colors do not tell you anything about a particular country. They are there to make it easier to see each country separately on the map. This type of map is called a political map because it shows the world's divisions by country.

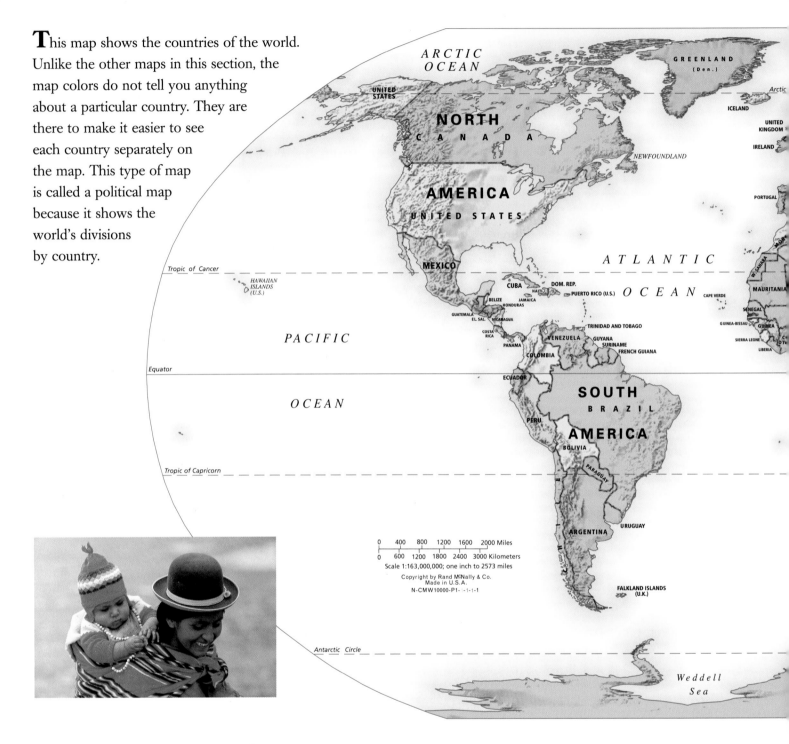

International boundaries are represented on this map by a dashed black line. These lines divide the world into separate countries. Sometimes country borders follow natural features such as rivers or mountain ranges. For example, the crooked northwestern border of China runs along a river. In many places, though, people decide where boundaries should fall—as with the straight portion of the boundary between Canada and the United States.

Although most political boundaries are well established, changes still occur. In 1990, for instance, East and West Germany reunited, and Germany became a single country. In 1991 the Soviet Union dissolved, and its 15 republics all became independent countries.

Some countries, like Russia and Canada, are large and take up a lot of space on any world political map. Other countries–like Vatican City in Rome, Italy– are so tiny that they aren't usually shown on a world political map unless the map scale is very large.

When people study the world, they often group countries by land areas called continents. The seven continents are the great divisions of Earth's land. Nearly all of them are landmasses almost completely surrounded by water.

This atlas divides the world into the seven continents: North America, South America, Europe, Africa, Asia, Australia (including the South Pacific area of Oceania), and Antarctica.

NORTH AMERICA

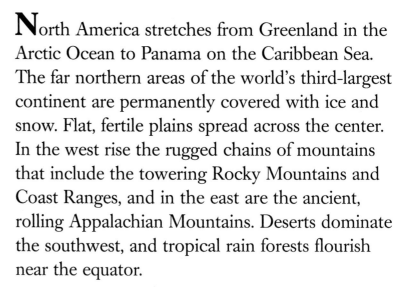

North America stretches from Greenland in the Arctic Ocean to Panama on the Caribbean Sea. The far northern areas of the world's third-largest continent are permanently covered with ice and snow. Flat, fertile plains spread across the center. In the west rise the rugged chains of mountains that include the towering Rocky Mountains and Coast Ranges, and in the east are the ancient, rolling Appalachian Mountains. Deserts dominate the southwest, and tropical rain forests flourish near the equator.

North America is a continent of spectacular scenery, varied landscapes, and vast resources. It includes the Canadian Shield, where Earth's oldest rock lies; the glacier-gouged Great Lakes; the breathtaking Grand Canyon; the endless expanses of Mexico's white-sand beaches, and the lush volcanic islands of the Caribbean.

New York (above) is the largest city in the United States; El Castillo (left) at Chichen Itza, Mexico, represents ancient Mayan architecture; the lofty Alaska Range (below) soars above clouds in Denali National Park.

Land Elevation
Feet (Meters)

- 9,840 and over (3,000 and over)
- 6,560 - 9,840 (2,000 - 3,000)
- 3,280 - 6,560 (1,000 - 2,000)
- 1,640 - 3,280 (500 - 1,000)
- 656 - 1,640 (200 - 500)
- 0 - 656 feet (0 - 200)

Scale 1:45,000,000; one inch to 710 miles
Copyright by Rand McNally & Co.
Made in U.S.A.
N-CMW20000-A1- -1- -1-1

North America Facts

Area: 9,500,000 square miles (24,700,000 square kilometers)

Highest Mountain: Mount McKinley, Alaska, United States, 20,320 feet (6,194 meters)

Lowest Point: Death Valley, California, United States, -282 feet (-86 meters)

Longest River: Mississippi-Missouri, central United States, 3,740 miles (6,019 kilometers)

Largest Lake: Lake Superior, Canada-United States 31,700 square miles (82,100 square kilometers)

Largest Desert: Chihuahuan Desert, Mexico-United States, 175,000 square miles (453,000 square kilometers)

Largest Island: Greenland, 840,000 square miles (2,175,600 square kilometers)—*world's largest island*

THE LAND

North America is a land of abundance. The continent has plentiful minerals, mighty rivers that provide hydroelectric power, and rich farmland that yields fruits, vegetables and grain. The United States is the economic powerhouse of the continent, while Canada's economy is also diversified with mining, agriculture, and tourism. Mexico's oil fields are one of that country's most important resources. The countries of Central America export a variety of tropical produce to lands farther north.

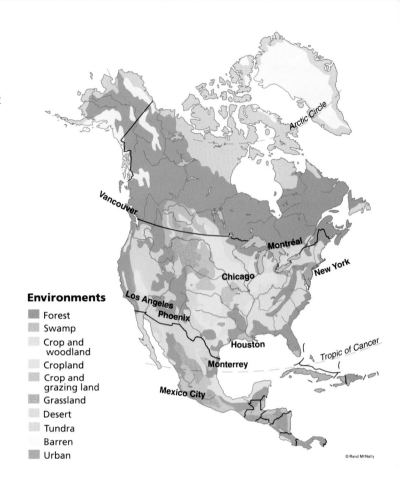

Environments

- Forest
- Swamp
- Crop and woodland
- Cropland
- Crop and grazing land
- Grassland
- Desert
- Tundra
- Barren
- Urban

© Rand McNally

Steel production in the United States and Canada is one of North America's best-known industries.

Industry
Industry provides a huge portion of the wealth in North America. Most industrial regions developed around port cities, where it was easy to receive raw materials and to ship out finished products. Mexico's role in manufacturing is growing as companies from the United States relocate their factories there. Canada and the United States, however, are still the leading industrial countries in North America.

Farming
North America produces more of the world's food than any other continent. In the temperate region that extends from southern Canada to northern Mexico, major crops include corn, wheat, and soybeans. Tropical and subtropical regions export bananas, cocoa, coffee, oranges, and other produce.

Environments
Forests, North America's dominant environment, cover one-third of the continent. Much of the land in the continent's midsection, especially the plains that lie between the Rocky Mountains and the Appalachian Mountains, is devoted to farming and livestock. Parched, barren deserts stretch across large parts of the southwestern United States and northwestern Mexico. Tundra spreads across most of Alaska and northern Canada. A thick sheet of ice covers nearly the entire island of Greenland. In contrast, the islands of the Caribbean support lush vegetation and dense tropical forests.

The midwestern United States is one of the world's largest producers of corn.

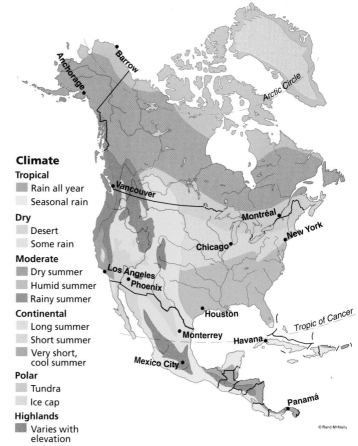

Economies

Economies	
	Little or no activity
	Nomadic herding
	Hunting, forestry, subsistence farming
	Forestry
	Agriculture
	Stock raising
	Manufacturing, commerce
	Fishing

Climate

Climate	
Tropical	
	Rain all year
	Seasonal rain
Dry	
	Desert
	Some rain
Moderate	
	Dry summer
	Humid summer
	Rainy summer
Continental	
	Long summer
	Short summer
	Very short, cool summer
Polar	
	Tundra
	Ice cap
Highlands	
	Varies with elevation

Economies

North America's abundant resources provide both the continent and the world with food, raw materials such as wood and mineral ores, and manufactured goods.

Mining and Mineral Resources

Much of the world's copper, lead, iron ore, and zinc are mined in North America. Coal, oil, and natural gas are plentiful, providing fuel for the factories of Canada, the United States, and Mexico.

Coal miners wear headlamps and protective gear when they work underground.

Climate

Almost every type of climate is found in North America, from the frozen tundra in the far north to the tropical areas in the south. Much of the continent, however, enjoys a temperate climate that is just right for growing crops and raising cattle.

A logger loads cut timber onto a truck for transport.

Forestry

Canada is one of the world's major exporters of wood and wood products. Forestry also plays a major role in the economies of the Pacific Northwest, the Gulf Coast, and the southern Atlantic coastal regions of the United States.

THE PEOPLE

North America is a land settled by immigrants. Even the earliest North American Indians migrated from Asia across a land bridge that once linked the two continents. Today, much of the population is descended from Europeans; African Americans, many of whose ancestors were brought to North America as slaves from the sixteenth to the nineteenth centuries, are also an important part of North America's ethnic mix. North Americans speak Spanish and English primarily; French is spoken in the Canadian province of Québec. Many other native languages are also spoken throughout the continent. The United States has the largest population of any country in North America, and Mexico City is the continent's most populous city.

Three cowboys in Mexico City prepare to ride in a rodeo.

Children laugh on a playground in Cuba.

Montréal, Canada, has a distinctly French character.

The Inuit people of Alaska and northern Canada build igloos with blocks of ice or compacted snow.

Los Angeles, California, reflects a "melting pot" of nationalities and cultures.

Three children row on a pond in New York's Central Park.

A costumed crowd gathers for a carnival on Antigua, an island in the Lesser Antilles.

ARCTIC OCEAN

Bering Sea

ALEUTIAN ISLANDS

Point Hope
Point Barrow
Beaufort Sea
Cape Bathurst

Arctic Circle

Nome
U.S.

Kuskokwim
Fairbanks
Mt. McKinley
20,320 ft.
Anchorage
Mt. Logan
19,524 ft.
Juneau
Gulf of Alaska
Alaska Peninsula
Alaska Range
Yukon
Bering Strait

QUEEN ELIZABETH ISLANDS
ELLESMERE ISLAND
Kap Morris Jesup
Kap Bridgman
GREENLAND (Denmark)
Arctic Circle
Kap Mostng
Godthab
Kap Farvel
Kap Mercy

DEVON ISLAND
BANKS ISLAND
VICTORIA ISLAND
Baffin Bay
Cape Adair
BAFFIN ISLAND

Mackenzie

Great Bear Lake
Great Slave Lake
Yellowknife
Churchill
Hudson Bay
Péninsule d'Ungava

QUEEN CHARLOTTE ISLANDS
VANCOUVER ISLAND

Peace
CANADA

Rocky
Edmonton
Vancouver
Calgary
Seattle
Regina
Saskatchewan
Lake Winnipeg
Winnipeg
Nelson
Albany
NEWFOUNDLAND
St. John's
Gulf of St. Lawrence
Cape Sable
Halifax

Columbia
Portland
Cape Blanco
Boise
Snake
Mountains
Missouri
Thunder Bay
Lake Superior
Quebec
MONTREAL
Ottawa
Toronto
Lake Huron
Lake Michigan
St. Paul
Minneapolis
Milwaukee
CHICAGO
DETROIT
Buffalo
Cleveland
Lake Ontario
Lake Erie
Boston
Cape Cod
NEW YORK
PHILADELPHIA

Cape Mendocino
San Francisco
Oakland
San Jose
Salt Lake City
Great Salt Lake
Great Basin
Sierra Nevada
Mt. Whitney 14,494 ft.
UNITED STATES
Omaha
Denver
Colorado
Kansas City
St. Louis
Pittsburgh
Louisville
Washington
Richmond
Norfolk
Arkansas
Ohio
Appalachian Mts.

LOS ANGELES
SAN DIEGO
Tijuana
Albuquerque
Phoenix
Tucson
Wichita
Tulsa
Nashville
Memphis
Charlotte
Cape Hatteras
ATLANTIC OCEAN
Red
El Paso
DALLAS
Fort Worth
Birmingham
Atlanta

Ciudad Juárez
San Antonio
HOUSTON
New Orleans
Mobile
Jacksonville
Rio Grande
Chihuahua
Tampa
Cape Canaveral

PACIFIC OCEAN
Punta Eugenia
Gulf of California
Baja California
Sierra Madre Occidental
Sierra Madre Oriental
MEXICO
Tropic of Cancer
Cabo San Lucas
MONTERREY
Tampico
GULF OF MEXICO
Cape Sable
Miami
BAHAMAS
Tropic of Cancer
HAVANA
GREATER ANTILLES
CUBA
DOMINICAN REPUBLIC
PUERTO RICO (U.S.)
LESSER ANTILLES

San Luis Potosí
GUADALAJARA
León
MEXICO CITY
PUEBLA
Acapulco
Mérida
Bahía de Campeche
Veracruz
Yucatan Peninsula
Pico de Orizaba 18,406 ft.
Canal de Yucatan
JAMAICA
Kingston
HAITI
Port-au-Prince
SANTO DOMINGO
ISLAS REVILLAGIGEDO
Belmopan
BELIZE
Gulf of Honduras
Guatemala
GUATEMALA
San Salvador
EL SALVADOR
HONDURAS
Tegucigalpa
NICARAGUA
Managua
Lago de Nicaragua
San José
COSTA RICA
Panamá
PANAMA
Golfo de Panamá
CARIBBEAN SEA
TRINIDAD AND TOBAGO

N
W E
S

North America Facts

Population: 472,600,000

Population Density:
50 people per square mile
(19 per square kilometer)

Most Populous Country:
United States,
271,490,000 people

Largest City:
Mexico City, Mexico,
19,100,000 people
(metropolitan area)

0   200   400   600 Miles
0 200 400 600 800 1000 Kilometers
Scale 1:45,000,000; one inch to 710 miles
Copyright by Rand McNally & Co.
Made in U.S.A.
N-CMW20000-P1- -1-1-1

Ottawa has been Canada's capital since 1857.

CANADA

Canada is the largest country in North America. A large portion of the land lies in the harsh regions of the far north, making it one of the most sparsely populated countries in the world. Most of Canada's people live in cities and towns near the country's border with the United States. In 1999, a new territory called Nunavut, which means "Our Land," was carved out of the eastern and northern portions of the Northwest Territories; it joined 10 provinces and two other territories. Most of the citizens of Nunavut are Inuit, the native people of northern Canada.

Totem poles are an integral part of Native American culture in western Canada.

On Prince Edward Island, a lighthouse stands at Shipwreck Point.

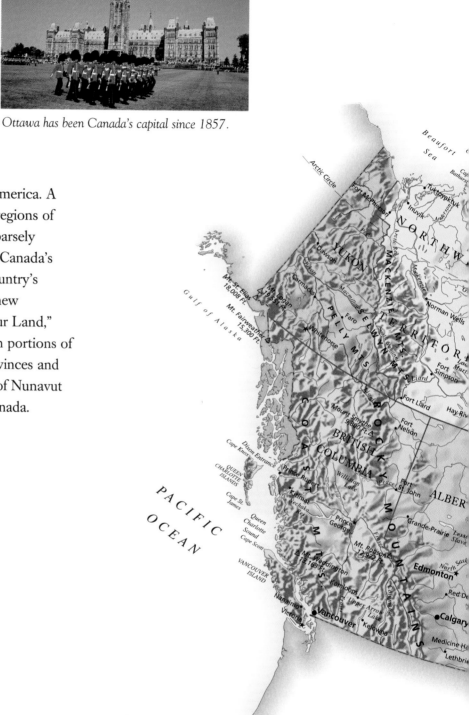

Polar bears roam the frozen wilderness of northern Canada.

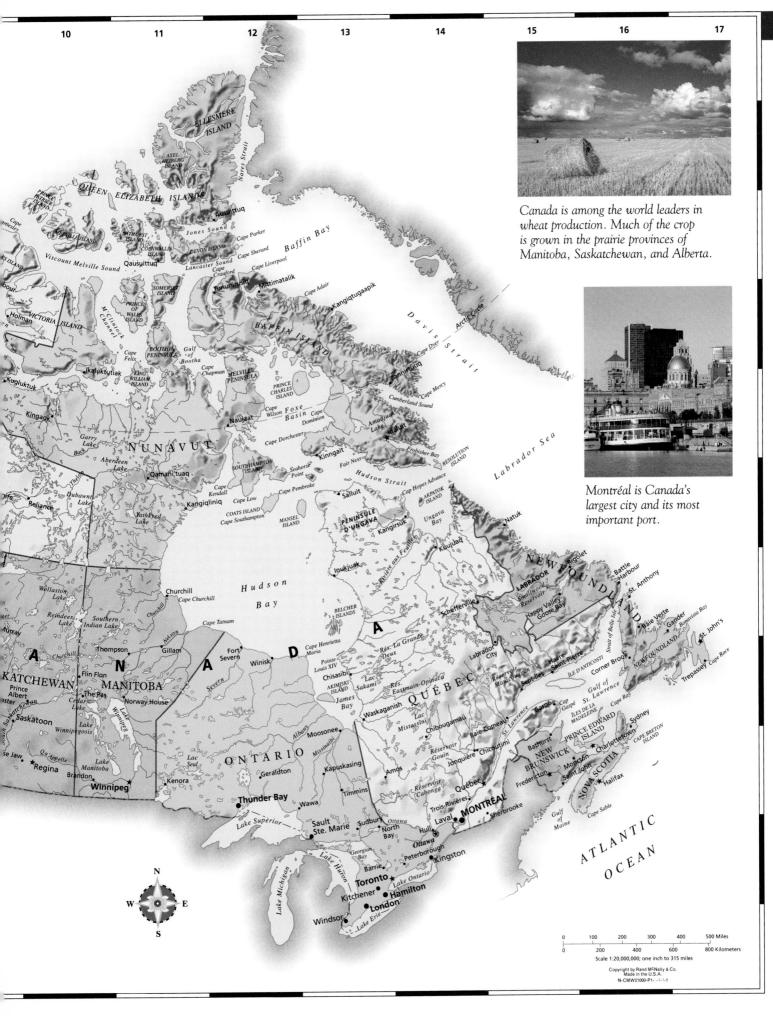

Canada is among the world leaders in wheat production. Much of the crop is grown in the prairie provinces of Manitoba, Saskatchewan, and Alberta.

Montréal is Canada's largest city and its most important port.

UNITED STATES

The United States occupies the central portion of the continent, but also includes Alaska, next to Canada's northwest corner, and Hawaii, a chain of islands in the middle of the Pacific Ocean. The United States is the most prosperous and populous country in North America. It also has the world's most ethnically diverse population. A large number of the country's people live in or near its many large cities. There are other areas, especially in the west, where the population is extremely sparse. The landscape of the United States is varied and beautiful, ranging from stark deserts and rocky canyons to majestic mountains and endless plains.

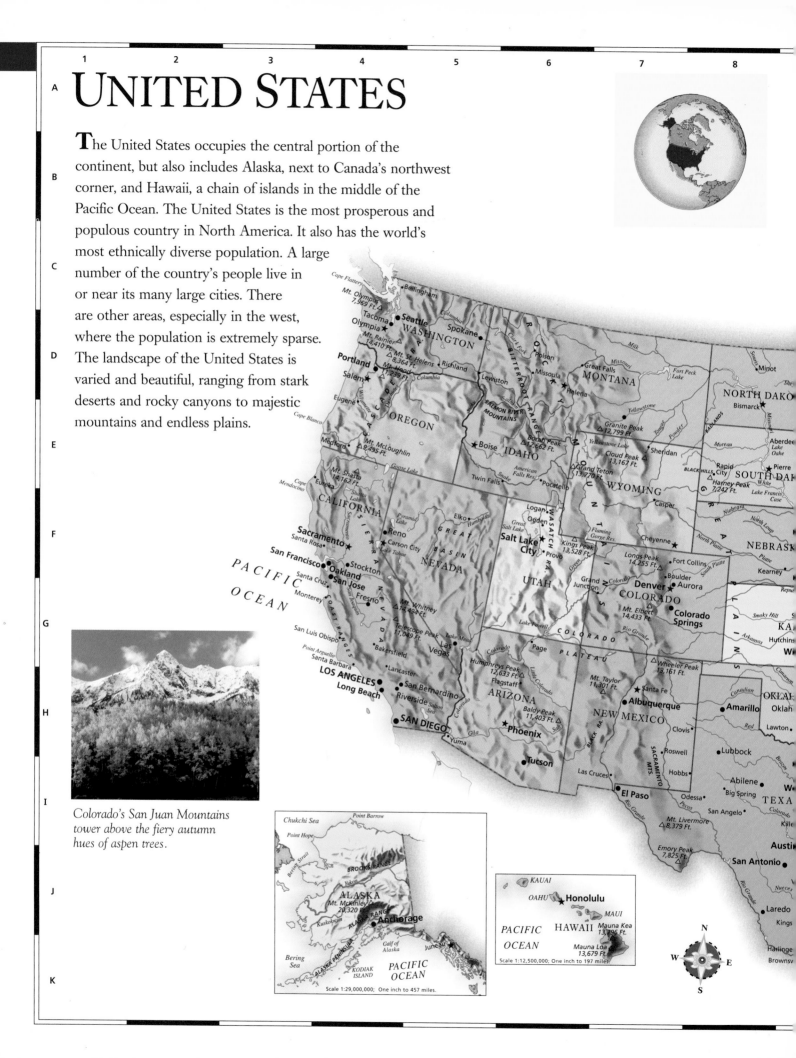

Colorado's San Juan Mountains tower above the fiery autumn hues of aspen trees.

1 2 3 4 5 6 7 8

A B C D E F G H I J K

Cape Flattery
Bellingham
Mt. Olympus 7,969 Ft. △
Tacoma • Seattle • Spokane
Olympia ★ WASHINGTON
Mt. Rainier △ 14,410 Ft.
Portland • Mt. St. Helens △ 8,364 Ft. • Richland
Salem ★ Mt. Hood △ 11,239 Ft.
Columbia
Eugene OREGON
Cape Blanco
Medford • Mt. McLoughlin △ 9,495 Ft.
Mt. Shasta △ 14,162 Ft.
Cape Mendocino Eureka •
Goose Lake
Shasta Lake
CALIFORNIA
Sacramento ★ Pyramid Lake
Santa Rosa • • Reno
San Francisco • Carson City
Oakland • Lake Tahoe
Santa Cruz • Stockton
San Jose •
Monterey • Fresno
San Luis Obispo
COAST RANGES
SIERRA NEVADA
Mt. Whitney △ 14,495 Ft.
Telescope Peak 11,049 Ft. △
Point Arguello
Santa Barbara • Bakersfield
Lancaster •
LOS ANGELES ★ • San Bernardino
Long Beach • Riverside • Salton Sea
SAN DIEGO ★
Yuma •
Colorado
Gila

Columbia
Clark Fork • Polson
Missoula •
BITTERROOT RANGE
SALMON RIVER MOUNTAINS
Salmon
Borah Peak △ 12,662 Ft.
★ Boise IDAHO
Twin Falls •
American Falls Res.
• Pocatello
Snake
Logan •
Ogden •
Great Salt Lake
Salt Lake City ★ WASATCH RA.
• Provo
NEVADA
Elko • Humboldt
GREAT BASIN
Las Vegas •
Lake Mead
Page •
Colorado
Grand Junction •
Kings Peak △ 13,528 Ft.
UTAH
Lake Powell
COLORADO PLATEAU
Humphreys Peak 12,633 Ft △
Flagstaff •
Mt. Taylor △ 11,301 Ft.
ARIZONA
Baldy Peak △ 11,403 Ft.
★ Phoenix
• Tucson
Little Colorado
BLACK RA.
NEW MEXICO
Albuquerque •
Santa Fe ★
Clovis •
Roswell •
Las Cruces •
SACRAMENTO MTS.
El Paso •

Great Falls •
MONTANA
Missouri
Fort Peck Lake
Helena ★
Milk
Yellowstone
Granite Peak △ 12,799 Ft.
Yellowstone Lake
Grand Teton △ 13,770 Ft.
Cloud Peak △ 13,167 Ft.
• Sheridan
WYOMING
Flaming Gorge Res.
Longs Peak △ 14,255 Ft.
• Cheyenne
• Fort Collins
Green
• Boulder
Denver ★ • Aurora
COLORADO
Mt. Elbert △ 14,433 Ft.
Colorado Springs •
Rio Grande
Wheeler Peak △ 13,161 Ft.
Canadian

NORTH DAKOTA
• Minot
Bismarck •
Missouri
BADLANDS
• Aberdeen
Lake Oahe
Moreau
• Pierre
BLACK HILLS
Rapid City • Harney Peak △ 7,242 Ft.
White SOUTH DAKOTA
Lake Francis Case
Niobrara
North Loup
North Platte
NEBRASKA
South Platte
Platte
• Kearney
Republi
Smoky Hill
KANSAS
Arkansas
Hutchins
Wi
Cimarron
OKLAHOMA
Oklah
• Amarillo
Lawton
Red
• Lubbock
• Abilene • Big Spring
TEXAS
Killeen
• San Angelo
Colorado
Mt. Livermore △ 8,379 Ft.
Pecos
• Odessa
Brazos
We
Austin
Emory Peak △ 7,825 Ft.
• San Antonio
Rio Grande
Nueces
• Laredo
Kings
Harlinge
Brownsv

Chukchi Sea
Point Barrow
Point Hope
Bering Strait
BROOKS RANGE
Yukon
ALASKA
Mt. Mckinley 20,320
ALASKA RANGE
Kuskokwim
• Anchorage
Gulf of Alaska
Bering Sea
ALASKA PENINSULA
KODIAK ISLAND
Juneau •
PACIFIC OCEAN
Scale 1:29,000,000; One inch to 457 miles.

KAUAI
OAHU
Honolulu ★
MAUI
PACIFIC OCEAN
HAWAII Mauna Kea 13,796 Ft.
Mauna Loa 13,679 Ft.
Scale 1:12,500,000; One inch to 197 miles.

PACIFIC OCEAN

N
W   E
S

10   11   12   13   14   15   16   17

The Navajo are one of many Native American tribes that live in the desert Southwest.

The design of many state capitol buildings imitates the dome shape of the U.S. Capitol in Washington, D.C.

Limestone-rich grasses in Kentucky contain a lot of calcium; horses that eat them often become strong runners.

Four surfers walk along the beach in southern California.

Prairie dogs make their homes in burrows across the central and western parts of the United States.

Scale 1:16,000,000; one inch to 252 miles.
Copyright by Rand McNally
Made in the U.S.A.
N-CMW24000-P1- .-.-.-1

MEXICO, CENTRAL AMERICA, AND THE CARIBBEAN

1 2 3 4 5 6 7 8

A B C D E F G H I J K

N
W E
S

Tijuana
Ensenada
Mexicali
BAJA CALIFORNIA
Nogales
Agua Prieta
Ciudad Juárez
Cerro de Encantada 10,069 Ft.
Gulf of California
ISLA CEDROS
Punta Eugenia
SONORA
Hermosillo
CHIHUAHUA
Ciudad Acuña
Empalme
Cuauhtémoc
Chihuahua
Piedras Negras
Volcán Las Tres Vírgenes 6,299 Ft.
Ciudad Obregón
Hidalgo del Parral
Delicias
Camargo
Nueva Rosita
BAJA CALIFORNIA SUR
Los Mochis
SIERRA MADRE OCCIDENTAL
COAHUILA
Nuevo Laredo
Monclova
Guasave
Guamúchil
San Pedro de las Colonias
NUEVO LEÓN
Frontera
Reynosa
Matamoros
La Paz
Culiacán
Gómez Palacio
Torreón
Saltillo
MONTERREY
Tropic of Cancer
Cabo San Lucas
Mazatlán
DURANGO
ZACATECAS
MEXICO
Linares
TAMAULIPAS
Durango
Ciudad Victoria
SINALOA
Matehuala
Fresnillo
SAN LUIS POTOSÍ
Ciudad Mante
GULF OF MEXICO
Zacatecas
Ciudad Madero
ISLAS MARÍAS
NAYARIT
AGUASCALIENTES
San Luis Potosí
Tampico
Aguascalientes
Ciudad Valles
ISLAS REVILLAGIGEDO
ISLA SAN BENEDICTO
Tepic
León
Cabo Rojo
ISLA ROCA PARTIDA
Puerto Vallarta
Guanajuato
Tuxpan
Mérida
ISLA SOCORRO
Tepatitlán
GUANAJUATO
Querétaro
Poza Rica
YUCATÁN
GUADALAJARA
Irapuato
QUERÉTARO
Martínez de la Torre
Campeche
YUCATÁN PENINSULA
JALISCO
Morelia
Pachuca
VERACRUZ
Ciudad Guzmán
Uruapan
HIDALGO
MEXICO CITY
TLAXCALA
Xalapa
QUINTANA ROO
COLIMA
Colima
MICHOACÁN
Toluca
MEXICO
Puebla
Veracruz
CAMPECHE
Chetumal
Tecomán
Cuernavaca
Pico de Orizaba 18,406 Ft.
Córdoba
Bahía de Campeche
Ciudad del Carmen
MORELOS
PUEBLA
Orizaba
TABASCO
Belize City
GUERRERO
Tehuacán
Coatzacoalcos
Villahermosa
Belmopan
SIERRA MADRE DEL SUR
Chilpancingo
Minatlán
BELIZE
Acapulco
Oaxaca
Gulf of Honduras
OAXACA
San Cristóbal de las Casas
San Pedro Sula
Juchitán
Tuxtla Gutiérrez
CHIAPAS
Golfo de Tehuantepec
Venustiano Carranza
GUATEMALA
El Progreso
Volcán Tajumulco 13,845 Ft.
GUATEMALA
HONDURAS
Tapachula
Tegucigalpa
Quezaltenango
Santa Ana
PACIFIC OCEAN
Escuintla
Sonsonate
Cojutepeque
San Miguel
San Salvador
Choluteca
EL SALVADOR
Chinandega
León
Managua

Roadrunner

Mexico, settled by Spaniards, has the largest Spanish-speaking population in the world. Most Mexicans live in cities—one-fourth of them in Mexico City alone. Mexico has large oil fields and silver deposits in its arid northern and western regions, and lush rain forests in the south, near the mountainous and densely forested countries of Central America. The "Mosquito Coast," along the Caribbean shore of Honduras, Nicaragua, and Costa Rica, is a sparsely populated land of swamps and abundant wildlife. Elsewhere in Central America, agriculture, especially coffee, beans, and bananas, is an important part of the economy. To the east of Mexico and Central America in the Caribbean Sea lie hundreds of coral and volcanic islands, inhabited by a vibrant mix of Africans, Asians, and Europeans. Many Caribbean islands are still controlled by the European countries that settled them centuries ago. The islands' coral-sand beaches and turquoise waters attract many tourists and cruise ships.

A bustling outdoor market in Guadalajara, Mexico, sells fruit, clothing, and toys.

10 11 12 13 14 15 16 17

A tugboat guides a tanker through the Panama Canal.

In Cuba, dominos is a common pasttime.

A T L A N T I C

O C E A N

GRAND
BAHAMA
ABACO
BAHAMAS
Nassau ELEUTHERA
NEW CAT ISLAND
PROVIDENCE
ANDROS
Tropic of Cancer
LONG ISLAND

Straits of Florida

HAVANA
Artemisa Matanzas Cárdenas
Güines
Pinar del Río Santa Clara Placetas
Cienfuegos Morón
Trinidad Florida
ISLA DE LA **CUBA** Camagüey Holguín Banes
JUVENTUD
Manzanillo Bayamo
Cabo Guantánamo
Cruz
CAYMAN ISLANDS
(U.K.)
George Town

W
E
S
T

MAYAGUANA
TURKS AND CAICOS ISLANDS
(U.K.)
ACKLINS
GREAT CAICOS
INAGUA ISLANDS *Grand Turk*

I N D I E S

Puerto
Plata
Cap-Haïtien San Francisco de Macorís VIRGIN **BRITISH**
Santiago ISLANDS **VIRGIN** **ANGUILLA**
Gonaïves **SANTO DOMINGO** (U.S.) **ISLANDS** (U.K.)
Santiago San Juan *San Juan* **ANTIGUA**
de Cuba La Romana *Caguas* **AND**
G **HAITI** Mayagüez Ponce ST. CROIX **BARBUDA**
R **Port-au-Prince** **PUERTO RICO** **ST. KITTS AND NEVIS** *St. John's*
Montego Bay E HISPANIOLA Barahona (U.S.) **MONTSERRAT** Pointe-à-Pitre
A **DOMINICAN** (U.K.) **GUADELOUPE**
Spanish Town T **REPUBLIC** Basse-Terre (Fr.)
JAMAICA *Kingston* **DOMINICA** *Roseau*
E **Fort-de-France**
R **MARTINIQUE**
(Fr.)
A Castries **ST. LUCIA** **BARBADOS**
N **ST. VINCENT** *Bridgetown*
T **AND THE**
I **GRENADINES** *Kingstown*
L
L **GRENADA**
E St. George's
S TOBAGO

C A R I B B E A N   S E A

L
E
S
S
E
R

A
N
T
I
L
L
E
S

ARUBA
(Neth.)
CARAGUA *Oranjestad* CURAÇAO **NETHERLANDS**
ANTILLES **Port of Spain**
BONAIRE **TRINIDAD AND TOBAGO**
Willemstad TRINIDAD
San Fernando

Cabo de Gracias a Dios

San José
uela
olcán Irazú Puerto Limón
Cerro Chirripó Golfo de los Colón
11,260 Ft. 12,530 Ft. Mosquitos *Panamá* **PANAMÁ**
A RICA La Chorrera **DE**
Volcán Barú David I S T M O Golfo de ISLA
11,401 Ft. **Panamá** DEL REY
Punta Burica Golfo de **PENÍNSULA** Punta Mala
Chiriquí **DE AZUERO**
ISLA DE COIBA Punta Mariato **PANAMA**

0 100 200 300 400 500 Miles
0 200 400 600 800 Kilometers
Scale 1:16,000,000; one inch to 252 miles
Copyright by Rand McNally & Co.
Made in U.S.A.
N-CMW30000-P1- -:-:-1

Tropical rain forests blanket much of Costa Rica.

Cabo San Lucas, at the southern tip of Mexico's Baja Peninsula, is known for its stunning rock arches.

SOUTH AMERICA

The architecture of Peru's Machu Picchu (above) reflects an advanced Inca culture; lush rain forests (below) cover Venezuela's Bolívar state; the toucan (right) lives in the rain forests of South America.

South America is a continent of geographical extremes, known for its tropical rain forests as well as the driest desert on Earth–the cold, desolate Atacama Desert in Chile. South America's northern border lies north of the equator on the Caribbean Sea. Its southernmost point at Cape Horn is only 600 miles (970 kilometers) from Antarctica. The Andes, which stretch along the entire western edge of the continent, form the longest mountain chain in the world. The highest peaks of the Andes are surpassed in height only by the Himalayas in Asia.

South America also boasts the world's largest river basin, the Amazon Basin; the world's highest waterfall, Angel Falls in Venezuela; and the world's highest lake used for transportation, Lake Titicaca on the border of Peru and Bolivia. Other principal landscape features include the broad plains of Bolivia and Paraguay's Gran Chaco and Argentina's Pampa, and the arid, rocky tablelands of Patagonia.

South America Facts

Area: 6,900,000 square miles (17,800,000 square kilometers)

Highest Mountain: Cerro Aconcagua, Argentina, 22,831 feet (6,959 meters)

Lowest Point: Salinas Chicas, Argentina, -138 feet (-42 meters)

Longest River: Amazon, 4,000 miles (6,400 kilometers)

Largest Lake: Lake Titicaca, Peru-Bolivia, 3,200 square miles (8,300 square kilometers)

Largest Desert: Atacama Desert, Chile, 57,000 square miles (148,000 square kilometers)

Largest Island: Tierra del Fuego, Chile-Argentina, 18,600 square miles (48,200 square kilometers)

Highest Waterfall: Angel Falls, Venezuela, 3,212 feet (979 meters)—*world's highest waterfall*

CARIBBEAN SEA

ATLANTIC
OCEAN

Punta
Gallinas

Pico Cristóbal Colón
18,947 Ft. △

CARACAS

Golfo
de
Panamá

Lago de
Maracaibo

Orinoco

Boca Grande

Llanos

VENEZUELA

GUYANA

Nev. del Tolima
17,110 Ft. △

BOGOTÁ

Pakaraima Mts.

SURINAME

FRENCH
GUIANA

Cabo Orange

Punta Magdalena

COLOMBIA

Nev. del Huila
18,865 Ft. △

Magdalena

Equator

Punta Galera

ECUADOR

△ Chimborazo
20,702 Ft.

Japurá

Negro

Amazon

MANAUS

Amazon

ÍLHA DE
MARAJÓ

Belém

Equator

Putumayo

Juruá

Madeira

Amazon

Basin

Tapajós

Tocantins

Punta Pariñas

GALAPAGOS
ISLANDS

Ucayali

Selvas

B R A Z I L

Cabo de
São Roque

A
n
d
e
s

P
E
R
U

Nev. Huascarán
22,133 Ft. △

RECIFE

Represa de
Sobradinho

LIMA

Nev. Illampu
△ 21,066 Ft.

Planalto do
Mato Grosso

Punta Carreta

Lago Titicaca

Cordillera Real

BOLIVIA

BRASÍLIA

São Francisco

PACIFIC

△ Nev. Sajama
21,463 Ft.

OCEAN

Ponta da Baleia

Tropic of Capricorn

ISLA SAN AMBROSIO

Nev. Ojos del Salado
22,615 Ft. △

Atacama Desert

Gran Chaco

PARAGUAY

Paraná

SÃO PAULO

RIO DE
JANEIRO

Cabo de São Tomé

Tropic of Capricorn

ISLA SAN FELIX

A
n
d
e
s

C
H
I
L
E

A
R
G
E
N
T
I
N
A

Paraná

Lagoa dos
Patos

ARCHIPIÉLAGO
JUAN FERNÁNDEZ

Cerro
Aconcagua
△ 22,831 Ft.

Santiago

P
a
m
p
a

URUGUAY

Lagoa Mirim

ATLANTIC

BUENOS
AIRES

Río de la Plata

OCEAN

Punta Lavapié

Cabo Quedal

Golfo San Matías

ISLA GRANDE
DE CHILOÉ

Península Valdés

ARCHIPIÉLAGO DE
LOS CHONOS

P
a
t
a
g
o
n
i
a

Cabo dos Bahías

Golfo San Jorge

Península
de Taito

Punta Medanoso

ISLA
WELLINGTON

FALKLAND ISLANDS
(U.K.)

Bahía
Grande

WEST
FALKLAND

EAST
FALKLAND

ISLA DESOLACIÓN

Strait of Magellan
TIERRA DEL
FUEGO

ISLA SANTA
INÉS

Cape Horn

Land Elevation
Feet (Meters)

	9,840 and over (3,000 and over)
	6,560 - 9,840 (2,000 - 3,000)
	3,280 - 6,560 (1,000 - 2,000)
	1,640 - 3,280 (500 - 1,000)
	656 - 1,640 (200 - 500)
	0 - 656 feet (0 - 200)

N
W   E
S

0 100 200 300 400 500 Miles
0   200 400 600 800 Kilometers
Scale 1:45,000,000; one inch to 710 miles

THE LAND

South America is known for its plentiful animal and plant life, most of which is found in the wilderness that covers a large part of the continent, from the jagged peaks of the Andes to the thick jungles of the Amazon Basin. Only about seven percent of the land is naturally suited for farming. South America is rich in mineral resources, but its industries are not well developed; most raw materials are exported and manufactured into products outside of the continent.

Brazil is one of the world's leading exporters of bananas.

Economies
- Little or no activity
- Nomadic herding
- Hunting, forestry, subsistence farming
- Forestry
- Agriculture
- Stock raising
- Manufacturing, commerce
- Fishing

© Rand McNally

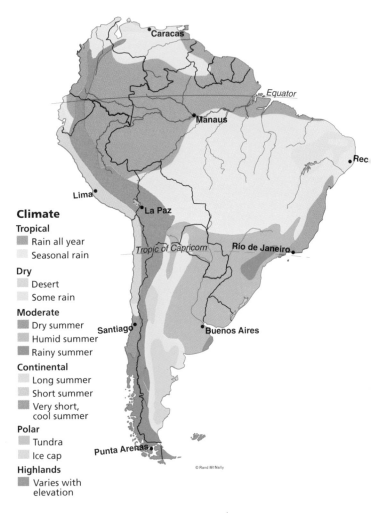

Climate

Tropical
- Rain all year
- Seasonal rain

Dry
- Desert
- Some rain

Moderate
- Dry summer
- Humid summer
- Rainy summer

Continental
- Long summer
- Short summer
- Very short, cool summer

Polar
- Tundra
- Ice cap

Highlands
- Varies with elevation

© Rand McNally

Economies

Stock raising, agriculture, and subsistence farming are important to South America's economy. Many parts of the rain forest have been burned out and cleared for farming, livestock grazing, and development. These slash-and-burn tactics have destroyed more than 200,000 square miles (518,000 square kilometers) of the Amazon rain forest in just 20 years. More than 40 square miles (103 square kilometers) vanish each day.

Climate

Tropical rain forest climates–hot and wet–and tropical savanna climates–hot with rainy and dry seasons–prevail in northern South America. Climates in the southern portion of the continent range from temperate, or moderate, to the subarctic chill of Tierra del Fuego. In parts of South America, the Andes block moist Pacific Ocean breezes from moving east, creating dry weather in the Patagonia region east of the mountains in Argentina and Chile. In other areas, the Andes rise alongside tropical regions.

Farming and Ranching

Many South Americans are involved in farming; some are subsistence farmers who grow only enough corn, beans, and potatoes to feed their families, while others work on huge commercial farms that produce crops for export. Cocoa, coffee, sugarcane, and bananas grow in abundance. Since much of the continent lies in the Southern Hemisphere—where the seasons are opposite those in the Northern Hemisphere—some countries export oranges, lemons, and grapes to the north during the northern winter. Vast cattle ranches dot the Gran Chaco of Bolivia and Paraguay, the Pampa of Argentina, and the Llanos of Venezuela and Colombia, while sheep graze the windswept landscapes of Patagonia and Tierra del Fuego.

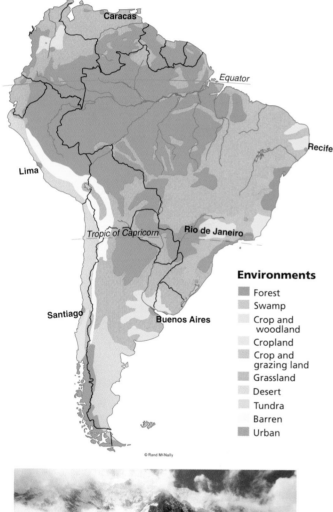

Environments

- Forest
- Swamp
- Crop and woodland
- Cropland
- Crop and grazing land
- Grassland
- Desert
- Tundra
- Barren
- Urban

© Rand McNally

Trekkers marvel at the beauty of Peru's snow-covered Andes.

Mining and Mineral Resources

Gold and silver, which drew Europeans to South America more than 500 years ago, are now mined in much smaller quantities than they once were. More than one-quarter of Earth's copper is buried in the Andes, where Chile's Chuquicamata, the world's most expansive open-pit mine, lies over the largest known copper deposit. Iron, bauxite, manganese, zinc, lead, oil, and natural gas are among the continent's important mineral resources.

Industry

While many of South America's industries remain underdeveloped, the more industrialized countries manufacture and process food, metals, chemicals, petroleum, textiles, clothing, cars, and appliances. Brazil is by far the leading industrial and economic producer on the continent, with Argentina, Venezuela, and Chile also contributing to the industrial sector.

Hundreds of oil rigs rise from the waters of Venezuela's Lake Maracaibo.

The Itaipu Dam on the Paraña River between Brazil and Paraguay provides hydroelectric power.

Tourism

Although tourism to cities such as Rio de Janeiro, Brazil, and Caracas, Venezuela, has declined in recent years, growing interest in adventure and nature-oriented travel is turning South America's more remote regions into prime vacation destinations. Travelers flock to study wildlife on the Galapagos Islands, experience history atop moss-covered Inca ruins high in the Andes, float down the Amazon, and trek through the starkly beautiful landscapes of Patagonia.

THE PEOPLE

Three girls in Peru wear the traditional clothing of the Quechua people.

The panpipe creates a distinctive sound in Ecuadorian music.

Rio de Janeiro celebrates Carnival every year with lavish costumes, music, and dancing.

South America's rich heritage comes from a vibrant combination of American Indian, European, and African peoples. From the sixteenth to the nineteenth centuries, Spain and Portugal controlled most of South America; today Spanish and Portuguese are the most widely spoken languages on the continent. Most South Americans live in crowded coastal cities–ninety percent of the population resides within 150 miles (240 kilometers) of the ocean. Native peoples, however, still dwell deep in the rain forests and the rugged high country. In the second half of the twentieth century, people from around the world immigrated to South America in search of new opportunities in trade and agriculture. Substantial Asian populations live in Brazil, Argentina, and Peru, for example. One of South America's most pressing social problems is the unequal distribution of wealth: A small percentage of rich people control most of the property, while great numbers of poor people crowd into makeshift shanty towns and squatter settlements called *favelas* that lie on the outskirts of the major cities.

Musicians serenade passers-by outside cafes and restaurants.

A Bolivian woman carries her baby on her back.

Two boys ride horses in Paraguay.

CARIBBEAN SEA

Punta Gallinas

Barranquilla MARACAIBO CARACAS
Cartagena Cúcuta Barquisimeto
Boca Grande

ATLANTIC
OCEAN

Orinoco *Llanos* VENEZUELA Georgetown
MEDELLÍN Bucaramanga GUYANA Paramaribo
Nev. del Tolima *Pakaraima Mts.* SURINAME Cayenne
17,110 Ft. BOGOTÁ FRENCH
Punta Magdalena COLOMBIA *Cabo Cacipore* GUIANA
CALI Boa Vista *Cabo Norte*
Nev. del Huila
18,865 Ft. Lérida
Punta Galera Macapá Equator
Equator QUITO *Cayambe* *ILHA DE* *Baía de Marajó*
18,996 Ft. *MARAJÓ*
ECUADOR *Nero* MANAUS Belém
GALÁPAGOS ISLANDS Iquitos *Japurá* Tefé Santarém São Luís
(Ecuador) GUAYAQUIL *Putumayo* *Amazon*
Punta Pariñas *Amazon* Imperatriz Teresina Fortaleza
Juruá *Tapajós* *Cabo de São Roque*
Chiclayo *Madeira* B R A Z I L Conceição do Natal
PERU Ji-Parana Araguaia *São Francisco* RECIFE
Nev. Huascarán *Planalto do* *Represa de*
22,133 Ft. *Mato Grosso* *Sobradinho* Feira Aracaju
Cusco Puerto Heath de Santana
Callao *Nev. Illampu* Cuiabá *Serra do Espinhaço* SALVADOR
LIMA 21,066 Ft. Goiânia BRASÍLIA Itabuna
Punta Carreta *Lago* LA PAZ Uberlândia *Represa de* *Ponta da Baleia*
Titicaca BOLIVIA *Tres Marias*
Arequipa Oruro Santa Cruz Campo
Nev. Sajama Sucre de la Sierra Grande BELO HORIZONTE
21,463 Ft. *Cabo de São Tomé*
PACIFIC Iquique *Gran Chaco* PARAGUAY *Paraná* Londrina
OCEAN SÃO RIO DE JANEIRO
Tropic of Capricorn Asunción PAULO Santo André
Antofagasta San Miguel Santa Florianópolis
Punta Ballenita de Tucumán Maria
ISLA SAN AMBROSIO *Nev. Ojos del Salado* *Paraná* *Lagoa dos* PORTO ALEGRE
(Chile) 22,615 Ft. Goya *Patos*
Punta Cachos CÓRDOBA Santa Fe URUGUAY *Lagoa Mirim*
ISLA SAN FÉLIX *Cerro* ROSARIO MONTEVIDEO
(Chile) Aconcagua
Valparaíso 22,831 Ft. BUENOS *Punta del Este*
ARCHIPIÉLAGO Santiago AIRES *Río de la Plata*
JUAN FERNÁNDEZ La Plata
(Chile) ATLANTIC
Concepción *Pampa* OCEAN
Punta Lavapié Mar del Plata
Valdivia Neuquén Bahía
Cabo Quedal Blanca
Golfo San Matías
ISLA GRANDE DE CHILOÉ *Península Valdés* N
ARCHIPIÉLAGO DE LOS CHONOS *Cabo dos Bahías* W E
Peninsula *Golfo San Jorge*
de Taitao Comodoro Rivadavia S
Punta Medanoso
ISLA WELLINGTON FALKLAND ISLANDS
Bahía *WEST* (U.K.)
Grande *FALKLAND* Stanley
Strait of Magellan *EAST FALKLAND*
TIERRA DEL
FUEGO
Punta Arenas
ISLA SANTA INÉS *Cape Horn*

0 100 200 300 400 500 Miles
0 200 400 600 800 Kilometers
Scale 1:45,000,000; one inch to 710 miles
Copyright by Rand McNally & Co. Made in U.S.A.
N-CMW40000-P1- -!-!-1

Copyright by Rand McNally & Co. Made in U.S.A.
N-CMW40000-P1- -!-!-1

South America Facts

Population:
340,000,000

Population Density:
49 people per square mile
(19 per square kilometer)

Most Populous Country:
Brazil, 170,860,000 people

Largest City:
São Paulo, Brazil,
17,200,000 people
(metropolitan area)

A Brazilian boy holds his pet dog.

CARIBBEAN SEA

PENÍNSULA DE LA GUAJIRA
Punta Gallinas
Punto Fijo
PENÍNSULA DE PARAGUANÁ
ISLA DE MARGARITA

Santa Marta
Barranquilla
Pico Cristóbal Colón
18,947 Ft.
Golfo de Venezuela
Coro
CARACAS
Porlamar
Carúpano

Cartagena
Valledupar
MARACAIBO
Barquisimeto
Valencia
Maracay
Barcelona
Cumaná

Sincelejo
Sahagún
Lago de Maracaibo
Valera
Acarigua
Valle de la Pascua
Anaco
Maturín
Tucupita
Orinoco

Monteria
Mérida
Pico Bolívar
16,427 Ft.
Guanare
Barinas
Calabozo
El Tigre
Cerro Bolívar
2,631 Ft.
Ciudad Guayana

Punta Marzo
Barrancabermeja
Cúcuta
San Cristóbal
Apure
San Fernando
Ciudad Bolívar
Embalse de Guri

Bello
Bucaramanga
Floridablanca
Arauca
VENEZUELA
Angel Falls
Mt. Ro

Quibdó
Itagüi
MEDELLÍN
La Dorada
Duitama
Meta
Cerro Yaví
8,009 Ft.
Puerto Ayacucho
Auyan Tepuy
9,678 Ft.
LA GRAN SABANA

Cabo Corrientes
Manizales
Nev. del Tolima
17,110 Ft.
Tomo
PAKARAIMA

ISLA DE MALPELO
(Colombia)
Pereira
Armenia
BOGOTÁ
Vichada
Cerro Marahuaca
8,461 Ft.

Punta Magdalena
Ibagué
Villavicencio
COLOMBIA
Guaviare
Orinoco
SIERRA PARIMA

Buenaventura
Palmira
Inírida
Boa Vista

CALI
Neiva
Guaviare

Nev. del Huila
18,865 Ft.
Popayán
Vaupés
SIERRA DE LA MACARENA
Icana

Tumaco
Cabo Manglares
Pasto
Florencia
Apaporis
SIERRA DE CURUPIRA

Esmeraldas
Ipiales
Ibarra
Vaupés
Lérida
Pico da Neblina
9,888 Ft.
Negro

Punta Galera
Equator
QUITO
Cayambe
18,996 Ft.
Caquetá
Branco

Cabo Pasado
Ambato
Putumayo
Japurá
AMAZON BASIN
MANA

GALÁPAGOS ISLANDS
(Ecuador)
Manta
Portoviejo
Chimborazo 20,702 Ft.
Napo
Içá
Amazon
Tefé
Manacapuru

Cabo San Lorenzo
Jipijapa
ECUADOR
Amazon

Punta Santa Elena
Milagro
Pastaza
Iquitos
Leticia

GUAYAQUIL
Cuenca
Tigre
Juruá

Golfo de Guayaquil
ISLA PUNÁ
Machala
Marañón
Içá

Tumbes
Loja
Ucayali
Jutaí
SELVAS

Talara
Sullana
Purus
Humaitá

Punta Pariñas
Piura
Jurua
Tapauá

Chiclayo
Cajamarca
Cruzeiro do Sul
Pucallpa
Purus

Trujillo
Huallaga
Madeira
Porto Velho

Chimbote
Huaraz
Nev. Huascarán
22,133 Ft.
Río Branco
Ariquemes

Nevado Yerupaja
21,765 Ft.
Huánuco
Cerro de Pasco
Acre
Ji-Paraná
Machado

Punta Lachay
Huacho
Ucayali
Orthon
Madre de Dios

Callao
Tarma
PERU
Río de las Piedras

LIMA
Vitarte
Huancayo
CORDILLERA ORIENTAL
Puerto Maldonado
Beni

Chinchay Alta
Ayacucho
Cusco
Mamoré
San Martín

Pisco
Ica
CORDILLERA DE HUANZO
Nevado Coropuna
20,686 Ft.
Trinidad

Punta Carreta
Nazca
Puno
Lago Titicaca
Nev. Illampu 21,066 Ft.
BOLIVIA
Santa Cruz de la Sierra

Volcán Misti
19,101 Ft.
Nev. Illimani 20,741 Ft.
Cochabamba
Montero

Punta Parada
CORDILLERA OCCIDENTAL
Arequipa
LA PAZ
CORDILLERA REAL

Volcán Tutupaca
19,898 Ft.
ALTIPLANO
Oruro
Sucre

Volcán Sajama
21,463 Ft.
Tacna
Lago Poopó
ANDES
Potosí

Tropic of Capricorn
Tarija

N
W   E
S

NORTHERN SOUTH AMERICA

Mountains and rain forests dominate the northern portion of South America. Besides the Andes, other highland areas rise in Guiana and Brazil, which lie north and south of the Amazon Basin, respectively. The tropical rain forests that fill the basins of the Amazon and Orinoco Rivers provide a home for more than 1,500 species of fish, 8,000 species of insects, and 1.6 million species of plants. In the Andes, many remnants of Inca culture, including the impressive ruins at Machu Picchu, have survived for centuries.

Tapirs are strong swimmers, but they can also move quickly through their jungle habitats.

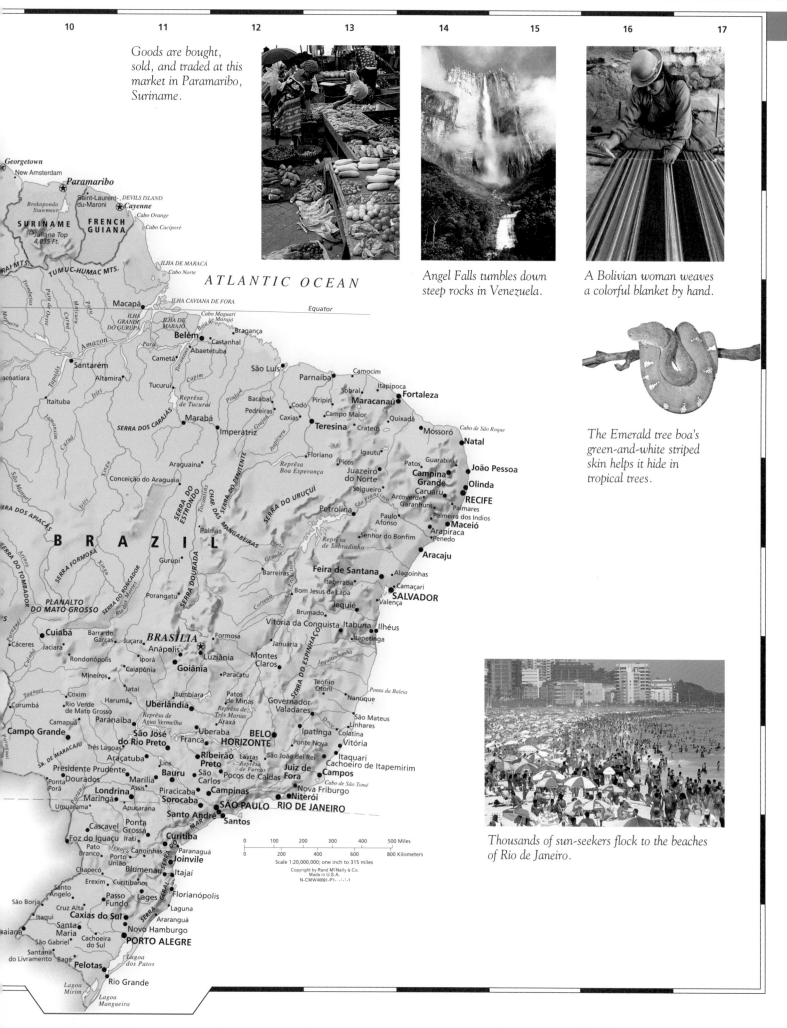

Goods are bought, sold, and traded at this market in Paramaribo, Suriname.

Angel Falls tumbles down steep rocks in Venezuela.

A Bolivian woman weaves a colorful blanket by hand.

The Emerald tree boa's green-and-white striped skin helps it hide in tropical trees.

Thousands of sun-seekers flock to the beaches of Rio de Janeiro.

Georgetown
New Amsterdam
Paramaribo
Saint-Laurent-du-Maroni   DEVILS ISLAND
Cayenne
Brokopondo
Stuwmeer
Cabo Orange
SURINAME   FRENCH
GUIANA
Cabo Caciporé
Juliana Top
4,035 Ft.
RAI MTS.
TUMUC-HUMAC MTS.
Trombetas
ILHA DE MARACÁ
Cabo Norte

ATLANTIC OCEAN

Macapá
ILHA CAVIANA DE FORA
Equator
Paru de Oeste
Curuá
Maecuru
Amazon
ILHA
GRANDE
DO GURUPÁ
Cabo Maguari
Baía de Marajó
ILHA DE
MARAJÓ
Bragança
Belém   Castanhal
Cametá   Abaetetuba
Acoatiara   Santarém   *Pará*   Camocim
Tapajós   Altamira   Tucuruí   São Luís   Parnaíba   Itapipoca
Itaituba   *Capim*   **Maracanaú**   **Fortaleza**
Iriri   *Xingu*   Bacabal   Codó   Piripiri   Sobral   *Cabo de São Roque*
Iguaçuzinho   *Curuá*   Represa   Pedreiras   Campo Maior   Quixadá
de Tucuruí   Marabá   Caxias   **Teresina**   Crateús   Mossoró
SERRA DOS CARAJÁS   Imperatriz   *Grajaú*   **Natal**
Floriano   Igautu
ERRA DOS APIACÁS   Araguaína   Picos   Guarabira
Conceição do Araguaia   Represa   Juazeiro   Patos   **João Pessoa**
Boa Esperança   do Norte   **Campina**   **Olinda**
SERRA DO   Selgueiro   **Grande**   Caruaru   **RECIFE**
Xingu   SERRA DO URUCUÍ   Arcoverde   Garanhuns
ERRA FORMOSA   ESTRONDO   Petrolina   Paulo   Palmares
Teles   Palmas   *São Francisco*   Afonso   Palmeira dos Indios
B R A Z I L   Gurupi   SERRA DAS MANGABÉIRAS   Arapiraca   **Maceió**
SERRA DO TOMBADOR   CHAP. DAS   Represa   Senhor do Bonfim   Penedo
PLANALTO   *Preto*   de Sobradinho   **Aracaju**
DO MATO GROSSO   SERRA DOURADA   Barreiras   Alagoinhas
Paraguai   Porangatu   **Feira de Santana**   Camaçari
Paraguai   Itaberaba   **SALVADOR**
Cuiabá   Barra do   *Correntinha*   Bom Jesus da Lapa   Valença
Cuiabá   Jaciara   Garças   Jucará   Formosa   **BRASÍLIA**   Jequié
Cáceres   Rondonópolis   Anápolis   *São Francisco*   Vitória da Conquista   Itabuna   Ilhéus
Iporá   **BRASÍLIA**   Montes   Itapetinga
Mineiros   Caiapônia   Luziânia   Claros   *Jequitinhonha*
Coxim   Jataí   **Goiânia**   Januária   SERRA DO ESPINHAÇO
Rio Verde   Itumbiara   Paracatu   Teófilo
Taquari   de Mato Grosso   Harumã   Ponta da Baleia
Corumbá   Patos   Nanuque
Camapuã   **Uberlândia**   de Minas   Governador
Campo Grande   Paranaíba   Represa de   Valadares   São Mateus
SA. DE MARACAJU   Três Lagoas   Água Vermelha   Araxá   Ipatinga   Linhares
São José   Uberaba   **BELO**   Colatina
Paraguai   Presidente Prudente   **do Rio Preto**   Franca   **HORIZONTE**   **Vitória**
Paraná   Dourados   Araçatuba   São   Ponte Nova   Itaquari
Ponta   Marília   Lins   Carlos   Lavras   São João del Rei   Cachoeiro de Itapemirim
Porã   Assis   **Bauru**   Pocos de Caldas   **Campos**
Londrina   Piracicaba   **Ribeirão**   *Doce*
Umuarama   Apucarana   **Preto**   Juiz de   Cabo de São Tomé
Maringá   **Campinas**   Fora
Cascavel   Ponta   **Sorocaba**   Nova Friburgo
Foz do Iguaçu   Grossa   **SÃO PAULO**   **RIO DE JANEIRO**
Pato   Canoinhas   **Santo André**   Niterói
Branco   Porto   **Curitiba**   **Santos**
União   Paranaguá
Chapecó   Joinville
Erexim   Blumenau   Itajaí
Santo   Curitibanos   Florianópolis
Angelo   Passo   Lages   Laguna
São Borja   Fundo
Itaqui   Cruz Alta   Araranguá
Caxias do Sul
Santa   Cachoeira
Maria   **Novo Hamburgo**   do Sul
São Gabriel   **PORTO ALEGRE**
Santana
do Livramento   Bagé   **Pelotas**
aiane   *Lagoa*
dos Patos
Rio Grande
Lagoa
Mirim
Lagoa
Manguera

0   100   200   300   400   500 Miles
0   200   400   600   800 Kilometers
Scale 1:20,000,000; one inch to 315 miles
Copyright by Rand McNally & Co.
Made in U.S.A.
N-CMW40091-P1- -1-1-1

SOUTHERN SOUTH AMERICA

Southern South America is shaped like a long cone. The Andes span the western side of this region, separating Chile from Argentina. The landscape includes the Atacama Desert to the west of the Andes, grasslands and dry tablelands to the east, and glaciers and fjords at the southernmost tip of the continent. Spanish is the main language here, but a few native groups continue to speak their own languages.

Grapes are grown in Chile and Argentina for food and for making wine.

Los Cuernos, a series of sculpted peaks, is one of the most spectacular sights in the southern Andes.

Asunción, Paraguay's capital city, still retains its Spanish colonial character.

Gauchos, or cowboys, have lived on the Pampa plains of Argentina for 300 years. They work on ranches and ride Criollos, a breed of wild horse.

Tango, the music and dance of Argentina, began in the slums of Buenos Aires.

Llamas are used for carrying goods up and down the steep slopes of the Andes.

In southern Uruguay, the town of Colonia del Sacramento borders the wide river called Rio de la Plata.

EUROPE

Europe is the second-smallest continent, but it shares the same landmass with another continent, Asia. Together, they are sometimes referred to as Eurasia.

The rounded mountains, deep fjords, and fertile plains of northern Europe were shaped by the glaciers that plowed across the region during past ice ages. Picturesque uplands and rugged mountains dominate the southern part of the continent. But the Alps in central Europe are the continent's most outstanding physical feature. These mountains began forming more than 60 million years ago when geologic forces pushed Africa northward toward Europe. The Great Northern European Plain arcs from the Pyrenees to the Urals, where Asia begins.

Switzerland's Matterhorn (above) is one of the highest peaks in the Alps; St. Basil's Cathedral (below) in Moscow, Russia, dates back to the 15th century; the scenic town of Cochem lies along the Mosel River in western Germany (below right).

ATLANTIC OCEAN

Reykjavik
Reykjanes
ICELAND
Hvannadalshnúkur
6,952 Ft.
Horn
Fontur

FAROE ISLANDS
(Den.)

ORKNEY
ISLANDS
SHE...
ISLA...

HEBRIDES

Moray
Firth
Grampian
Mts.
Kinnaird Head

UNITED
Firth of Forth
NOR...
KINGDOM

Cheviot
Hills

IRELAND
Irish
Sea

Mizen
Head

St. George's Channel

GREAT
BRITAIN

Land's End

Thames
LONDON

NE...
LA...

English Channel
CHANNEL IS.

Strait of Dover

BEL...

Paris
PARIS
Paris
Basin

Loire

Seine

FRANCE

Bay of Biscay

Cabo de Fisterra

Massif
Central

Mt. B...
15,771

Cordillera Cantabrica

Pyrenees

ANDORRA

Golfe du Lion

MO...

Duero

Ebro

Iberian
Peninsula

Sistema Ibérico

PORTUGAL

Lisbon

Tagus

SPAIN

Cabo de São Vicente

Sierra Morena

BALEARIC ISLANDS

MENORCA

EIVISSA

MALLORCA

Strait of Gibraltar

Cap de
la Nau

Mulhacén
11,424 Ft.

GIBRALTAR
(U.K.)

N
W · E
S

Nordkapp

Murmansk

Kol'skiy poluostrov

Ponoy

LOFOTEN

Arctic Circle

Kebnekaise 6,926 Ft.

Torneälven

Muonio

Lapland

White Sea

Mezen'

Pechora

Ural Mountains

NORWEGIAN SEA

Scandinavian Peninsula

NORWAY SWEDEN

Umeälven

FINLAND

Gulf of Bothnia

Severnaya Dvina

Onega

Kamskoye vdkhr.

Galdhøpiggen 8,100 Ft.

Kardelva

Glåma

Kebnes

ÅLAND

Ladozhskoye ozero

Onezhskoye ozero

Northern Uvals

Sukhona

Kama

RUSSIA

Stockholm

Vänern

Vättern

SAAREMAA

GOTLAND

ÖLAND

Gulf of Finland

ESTONIA

Chudskoye ozero

Rybinskoye vodokhranilishche

Gor'kovskoye vodokhranilishche

Kuybyshevskoye vodokhranilishche

Skagerrak

Kattegat

DENMARK

Copenhagen

BORNHOLM (DEN.)

BALTIC SEA

Gulf of Riga

Riga

LATVIA

LITHUANIA

Valdai Hills

MOSCOW

Oka

Khopër

Volga Hills

Volgogradskoye vdkhr.

RUSSIA

Neman

MINSK

Central Russian Upland

Don

Tsimlyanskoye vodokhranilishche

Volga

Great Northern European Plain

BELARUS

BERLIN

Elbe

Oder

GERMANY

POLAND

WARSAW

Wisła

Pripyat

Dnieper Lowland

Donets Basin

Ore Mts.

Sudetes

CZECH REPUBLIC

Bohemian Forest

KIEV

Dniester

UKRAINE

Dnieper

CASPIAN SEA

Lake Constance

Danube

SLOVAKIA

Carpathian Mountains

LIECH.

AUSTRIA

Grossglockner 12,461 Ft.

HUNGARY

Great Hungarian Plain

MOLDOVA

Sea of Azov

gora El'brus 18,510 Ft.

Caucasus

ERLAND

ALPS

SLOVENIA

Drava

CROATIA

Po

ROMANIA

Carpaţii Meridionali

Crimean Peninsula

Apennines

SAN MARINO

BOSNIA AND HERZEGOVINA

Dinaric Alps

YUGOSLAVIA

Balkan

Danube

BLACK SEA

ADRIATIC SEA

Peninsula

ROME

ITALY

Vesuvius 4,190 Ft.

BULGARIA

MACEDONIA

Rhodope Mts.

TYRRHENIAN SEA

ALBANIA

Pindhos Oros

Mt. Olimbos 9,570 Ft.

Mt. Etna 10,902 Ft.

SICILY

Capo Passero

IONIAN SEA

GREECE

Athens

AEGEAN SEA

MALTA

MEDITERRANEAN SEA

CRETE

RÓDHOS

Land Elevation: Feet (Meters)

9,840 and over (3,000 and over)	3,280 - 6,560 (1,000 - 2,000)
6,560 - 9,840 (2,000 - 3,000)	1,640 - 3,280 (500 - 1,000)
656 - 1,640 (200 - 500)	
0 - 656 feet (0 - 200)	

0   100   200   300   400   500 Miles
0   200   400   600   800 Kilometers

Scale 1:16,000,000; one inch to 252 miles
Copyright by Rand McNally & Co.
Made in U.S.A.
N-CMW50000-A1- -1-1-1

Europe Facts

Area: 3,800,000 square miles (9,900,000 square kilometers)

Highest Mountain: gora El'brus, Russia, 18,510 feet (5,642 meters)

Lowest Point: Caspian Sea, Russia, -92 feet (-28 meters)

Longest River: Volga, Russia, 2,290 miles (3,685 kilometers)

Largest Lake: Caspian Sea, Europe-Asia, 143,240 square miles (370,990 square kilometers)

Largest Island: Great Britain, 88,795 square miles (229,978 square kilometers)

THE LAND

Europe has a mild climate, a wealth of natural resources, and numerous rivers that have contributed to smooth and profitable trade between countries for centuries. These factors have also made European countries some of the wealthiest in the world. Most are able to sustain mixed economies based on many types of trade and manufacture, rather than only one or two.

Soaring, jagged peaks provide a striking backdrop for hikers in the French Alps.

Economies

European countries have traded freely with each other since the 1950s, when the first common market was established. More recently, the countries of eastern Europe have also begun competing in the open marketplace. In 1999, the European Union introduced the Euro, a unit of money that can be used in all member countries.

Economies

- Little or no activity
- Nomadic herding
- Hunting, forestry, subsistence farming
- Forestry
- Agriculture
- Stock raising
- Manufacturing, commerce
- Fishing

Environments

- Forest
- Swamp
- Crop and woodland
- Cropland
- Crop and grazing land
- Grassland
- Desert
- Tundra
- Barren
- Urban

Environments

Europe's environments range from frozen tundra and jagged mountains to grasslands and balmy beaches. Heavy industry and large human populations have polluted many land areas and waterways, but clean-up efforts are underway.

Arctic Circle

Stockholm

Moscow

London

Paris

Bucharest

Madrid

Rome

© Rand McNally

Arctic Circle

Murmansk

Arkhangel'sk

Stockholm

Moscow

Volgograd

London

Paris

Belgrade

Bucharest

Madrid

Rome

© Rand McNally

Climate

Tropical
- Rain all year
- Seasonal rain

Dry
- Desert
- Some rain

Moderate
- Dry summer
- Humid summer
- Rainy summer

Continental
- Long summer
- Short summer
- Very short, cool summer

Polar
- Tundra
- Ice cap

Highlands
- Varies with elevation

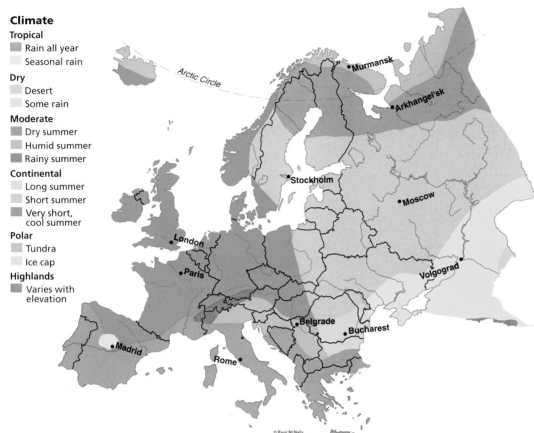

Climate

In western Europe, warm ocean air creates a climate far milder than northern lands elsewhere in the world. The currents don't affect eastern Europe, which experiences very cold winters. The Mediterranean climate of southern Europe has mild, wet winters and hot, dry summers.

In Denmark, a worker unloads a catch of sand eels from the North Sea.

Mining and Manufacturing

Europe's abundance of mineral resources, especially its coal, iron, and nickel reserves, fueled the Industrial Revolution of the 18th and 19th centuries and continues to supply the continent's industries today.

Germany is well-known for manufacturing automobiles with state-of-the art equipment.

Fishing and Farming

Western Europe's deeply etched coastline has long encouraged a healthy fishing industry. The European Plain supports some of the world's most fruitful farmland, while the climates and soils in Portugal, France, and Italy are perfect for growing grapes for fine wine.

Tourism

Thanks to their rich histories, pleasant climates, and stunning scenery, European countries are very popular tourist destinations. Today, many countries derive most of their income from tourist spending.

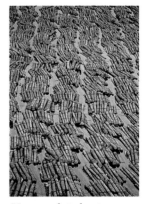

Tourists and natives enjoy the atmosphere of an outdoor cafe in Paris.

Forestry

Europe used to be covered with trees, but over the centuries many forests have been cleared for farms, cities, and manufacturing plants. There are still vast forests in Norway, Sweden, and Finland, which have large paper and wood-products industries.

Harvested timber is transported on inland waterways to mills, where it is processed.

THE PEOPLE

Although farming is an important part of Europe's economy, most Europeans live and work in cities. Europe may be a small continent, but its more than 40 countries feature a tremendous diversity of cultures. Differences in language, customs, food, clothing, and religion give each European country a distinct identity. In places such as Italy and Spain, regions within the same country have very different cultures.

Bullfighter in Spain

For much of its history, Europe has been a hotbed of wars and border disputes. Two world wars wracked the continent in the first half of the 20th century and left it divided into two major parts: the western capitalist countries and the eastern Communist countries, which were loosely controlled by the Soviet Union. After the 1991 breakup of the Soviet Union, countries in eastern Europe began to reunite with the politically and economically stable west, a process that has spawned more wars and social and ethnic unrest in many places.

Hungarian dancers celebrate Constitution Day in Budapest.

Guards at the Tower of London are known as "Beefeaters."

Meals in Italy's restaurants are often served outdoors.

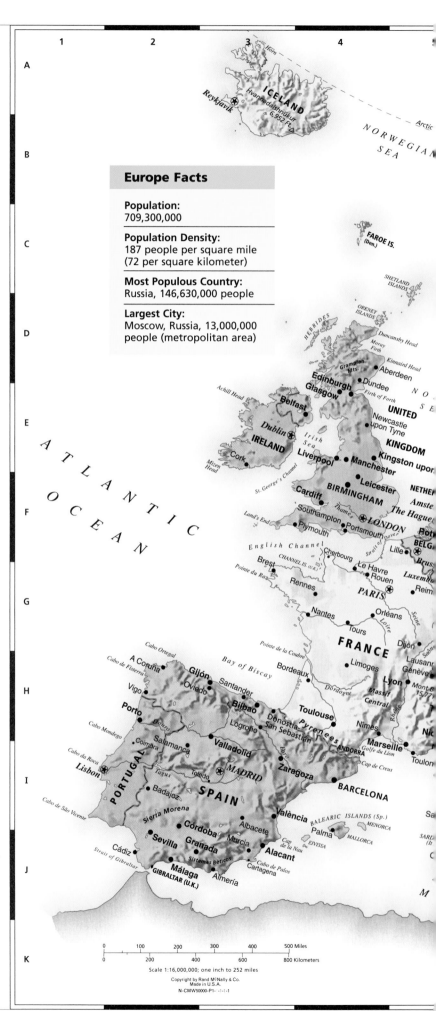

Europe Facts

Population:
709,300,000

Population Density:
187 people per square mile
(72 per square kilometer)

Most Populous Country:
Russia, 146,630,000 people

Largest City:
Moscow, Russia, 13,000,000 people (metropolitan area)

Scale 1:16,000,000; one inch to 252 miles

Copyright by Rand McNally & Co.
Made in U.S.A.
N-CMW50000-P1- -|-|-1

A Greek fisherman mends a handmade net.

NORTHERN EUROPE

Northern Europe is a land of surprising contrasts. North of the Arctic Circle, in parts of Scandinavia—Sweden, Norway, and Finland—some land is permanently frozen, while small palm trees dot beaches on Great Britain's southwestern coast. Vast portions of Iceland lie under *Vatnajokull*, a sheet of ice larger than all of Europe's other glaciers combined, while energy from Iceland's 250 hot springs and volcanic vents powers Reykjavik, the capital city. The Scandinavian countries are among the most sparsely populated in Europe, but the United Kingdom, which includes England, Scotland, Wales, and Northern Ireland, is one of the most densely populated. To the east, on the Baltic Sea, the countries of Latvia, Lithuania, and Estonia were once part of the former Soviet Union.

NORWEGIAN SEA

ATLANTIC OCEAN

Arctic Circle
Horn
GRÍMSEY
Breiðafjörður
Rifstangi
SNÆFELLSNES
Akureyri
Fontur
Faxaflói
ICELAND
Hvannadalshnúkur 6,952 Ft.
Reykjavík
REYKJANES
Hekla 4,892 Ft.
Djúpivogur
Stokksnes

Tromsø
VESTERÅLEN
LOFOTEN
Kebnekaise 6,926 Ft.
Kiruna
Malmb
Bodø
Mosjøen
Steinkjer
Östersund
Omskö
Trondheim
Helagsfjället 5,892 Ft.
Ålesund
Ljungan
Hull
Dombås
Otta
SWEDEN
Galdhøpiggen 8,100 Ft.
NORWAY
Lillehammer
Falun
Sognafjorden
Borlänge
Dalälven
Sar
Bergen
Lågen
Oslo
Lillestrøm
Västerås
Stoc
Haugesund
Drammen
Skien
Örebro
Eskilstuna
Stavanger
Porsgrunn
Sandefjord
Katrineholm
Motala
Nor
Uddevalla
Skövde
Linkö
Kristiansand
Trollhättan
Jönköping
Lindesnes
Vänern
Göteborg
Borås
Vetlanda
Skagerrak
Grenen
Varberg
Värnamo
Oskars
Frederikshavn
Ålborg
Ljungby
Kalmar
Viborg
Randers
Halmstad
Holstebro
Århus
Helsingborg
Karls
DENMARK
Kattegat
Copenhagen
Malmö
Trelleborg
BORNHOLM (Den.)
Kolding
SJÆLLAND
Esbjerg
Odense
Næstved
Rønne
Nykøbing
Kap Arkona
LOLLAND
BAL

FAROE ISLANDS (Den.)
Tórshavn

SHETLAND ISLANDS
RONA
Lerwick

ROCKALL (U.K.)

ORKNEY ISLANDS
Cape Wrath
Duncansby Head
HEBRIDES
The Minch
Inverness
Moray Firth
Kinnaird Head
Ben Nevis 4,406 Ft.
GRAMPIAN MTS.
SCOTLAND
Aberdeen
BRITISH ISLES
Perth
Stirling
Dundee
Firth of Forth
Glasgow
Edinburgh
UNITED
Malin Head
Londonderry
Kilmarnock
Ayr
GREAT BRITAIN
Bloody Foreland
Ballymena
Dumfries
CHEVIOT HILLS
Erris Head
NORTHERN IRELAND
Bangor
Stranraer
Carlisle
Donegal Bay
Belfast
Newcastle upon Tyne
Achill Head
ISLE OF MAN (U.K.)
Whitehaven
Sunderland
Galway
Dundalk
Middlesbrough
Irish Sea
Scarborough
NORTH SEA
Dublin
Bradford
York
KINGDOM
IRELAND
Liverpool
Manchester
Kingston upon Hull
Loop Head
Chester
Sheffield
Carrauntoohil 3,406 Ft.
Stoke on Trent
ENGLAND
Limerick
Derby
Nottingham
Norwich
Cork
Waterford
Shrewsbury
Leicester
Great Yarmouth
Mizen Head
BIRMINGHAM
Coventry
St. George's Channel
WALES
Hereford
Northampton
Cambridge
Milford Haven
Swansea
Newport
Oxford
Ipswich
CELTIC SEA
Cardiff
Bristol
Reading
Thames
LONDON
Hartland Point
Southampton
Dover
St. Austell
Exeter
Bournemouth
Brighton
Strait of Dover
ISLES OF SCILLY
Land's End
Plymouth
Portsmouth
Lizard Point
Start Point
English Channel
GUERNSEY (U.K.)
CHANNEL IS.
JERSEY (U.K.)
Golfe de St. Malo

Under the watchful eye of a shepherd, sheep graze on the green hills of Ireland.

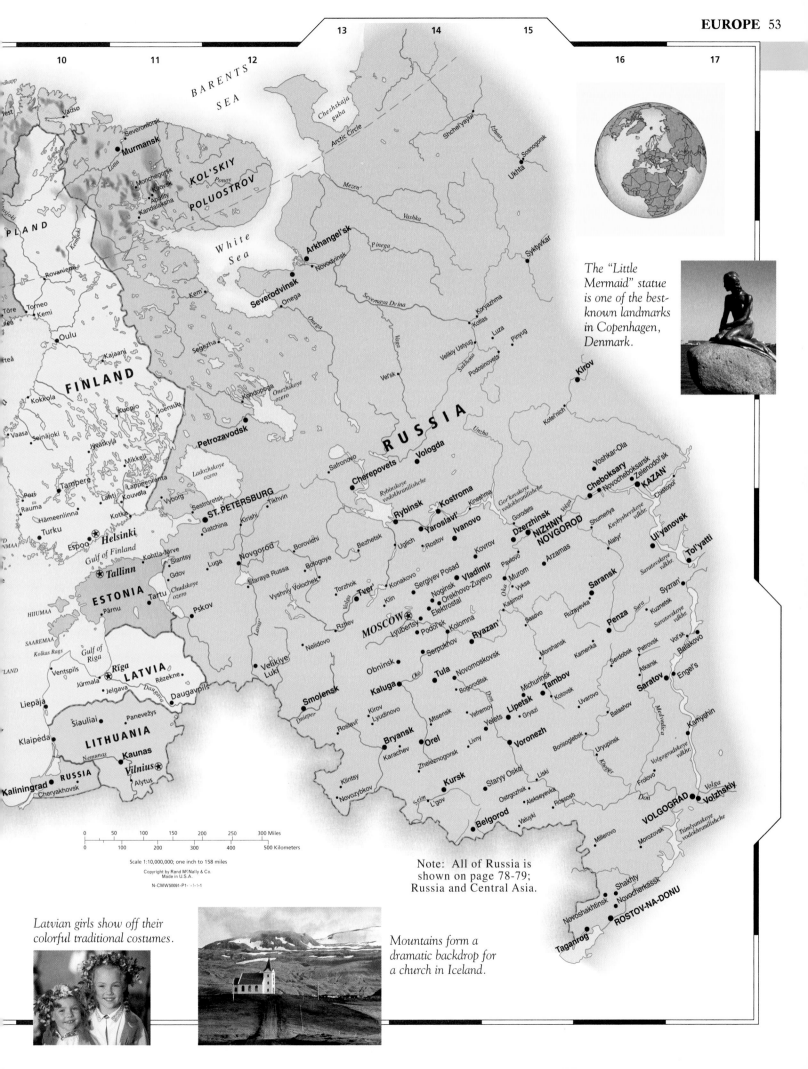

The "Little Mermaid" statue is one of the best-known landmarks in Copenhagen, Denmark.

Note: All of Russia is shown on page 78-79; Russia and Central Asia.

Scale 1:10,000,000; one inch to 158 miles

Copyright by Rand McNally & Co.
Made in U.S.A.

N-CMW50091-P1- -1-1-1

Latvian girls show off their colorful traditional costumes.

Mountains form a dramatic backdrop for a church in Iceland.

WESTERN AND CENTRAL EUROPE

Portuguese fisherman work on their nets before heading out to sea.

The cultures of western and central Europe are numerous and diverse, from the Islamic flavor of Spain's ancient Moorish cities to the sophisticated atmosphere of chic boutiques and sidewalk cafes in Paris, France. The region includes both the stunning beauty of the Swiss Alps and the heavy industry of Germany's Ruhr Valley. The slow, simple pace of life in a picturesque Italian hill town stands in contrast to the frenzied activity in the financial and political centers of Belgium and the Netherlands. Some of the smallest countries in the world are in this region: Andorra, San Marino, Monaco, and Vatican City, which is a tiny country entirely surrounded by the city of Rome, Italy.

Schönbrunn Palace in Vienna, Austria, was built for the Hapsburgs, a family that once ruled Austria, Germany, Spain, and other parts of Europe.

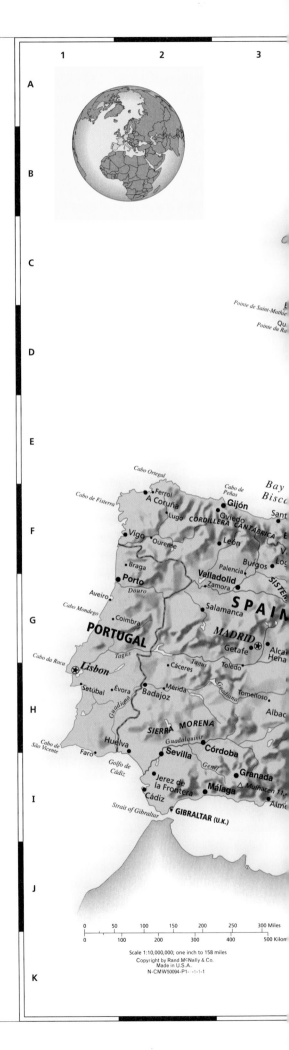

An Italian farmer inspects his grape crop.

The Colosseum in Rome was built nearly 2,000 years ago.

During the annual Grand Prix, racecars speed through the streets of Monte Carlo in Monaco.

Ibexes, a type of wild goat, graze on a hillside in Switzerland.

EASTERN EUROPE

In recent years, great changes have swept across Eastern Europe. From 1989 to 1991, the country known as the Soviet Union broke apart, and all 15 of its former republics–including Belarus, Ukraine, and Moldova–became independent countries. Then, in 1993, the country called Czechoslovakia split into two separate countries: the Czech Republic and Slovakia. These newly independent republics have worked to prosper in free market trade. Industry is thriving in Poland and Hungary, while others republics like Moldova and Slovakia remain largely agricultural.

Prague, in the Czech Republic, is one of Europe's loveliest and most historic cities.

The farmlands of Ukraine produce such bountiful harvests that this region is often referred to as the "Breadbasket of Europe."

Although the Carpathian Mountains skirt the borders of Poland, Slovakia, and Ukraine, most of Eastern Europe lies on the Great Northern European Plain where there is an abundance of fertile land. The beauty and mild weather of the Crimean Peninsula, which juts into the Black Sea, makes Ukraine a popular beach destination for tourists.

The Tatra Mountains are the primary range of the Carpathian Mountains.

Kiev, the capital of Ukraine, straddles both sides of the Dnieper River.

Hungary's Magyar people have been breeding horses for centuries.

Since World War II, Poland has had few minority groups. Today, its people have a very strong national identity.

BALTIC SEA

POLAND

WARSAW

Gdynia
Gdańsk
Koszalin
Elbląg
Suwałki
Tczew
Szczecin
Olsztyn
Grudziądz
Bydgoszcz
Toruń
Gorzów
Wielkopolski
Włocławek
Wisła
Poznań
Warta
Zielona Góra
Głogów
Kalisz
Łódź
Legnica
Piotrków
Trybunalski
Radom
Wrocław
Częstochowa
Kielce
SUDETES
Wałbrzych
Liberec
Opole
Cheb
Kladno
PRAGUE
Bytom
Sosnowiec
Kraków
CZECH REPUBLIC
Šumperk
Ostrava
Katowice
Bielsko-Biała
Plzeň
Písek
Olomouc
České
Budějovice
Brno
Kraków
CARPATHIAN MOUNTAINS
Žilina
Trenčín
Poprad
Prešov
Prievidza
Košice
Trnava
Banská
Bystrica
SLOVAKIA
Bratislava
Győr
Miskolc
Uzhhorod
Berehove
Gyöngyös
Nyíregyháza
Székesfehérvár
BUDAPEST
Kecskemét
HUNGARY
Debrecen
Kaposvár
Szeged
Dráva
Pécs
Danube
Tisza

BOHEMIAN FOREST

Polatsk
Vitsyebsk
Maladzyechna
Barysaw
Orsha
MINSK
Mahilyow
Hrodna
Lida
Krychaw
BELARUS
Neman
Baranavichy
Babruysk
Bialystok
Slonim
Slutsk
Homyel'
Łomża
Dniaper
Siedlce
Kobryn'
Pinsk
Pripyat
Mazyr
Brest
Hlukhiv
Zakh. Buh
Lublin
Kovel'
Chernihiv
Chełm
Spr
Korosten'
Chornobyl'
Konotop
Sumy
Luts'k
Rivne
Nizhyn
Pryluky
Dubno
Zhytomyr
KIEV
Okhtyrka
KHARKIV
L'viv
Berdychiv
Lubny
Kupians'k
Bila Tserkva
Poltava
Ternopil'
UKRAINE
Izium
Ivano-Frankivs'k
Khmel'nyts'kyi
Sieverodonets'k
Krosno
Sambir
Vinnytsia
Kremenchuts'ke vdskh.
Kremenchuk
Slovians'k
Luhans'k
Kamianets'-Podil's'kyi
Uman'
Oleksandriia
Kramators'k
Chernivtsi
Mohyliv-
Podil's'kyi
Kirovohrad
Dniprodzerzhyns'k
Stakhanov
Horlivka
Alchevs'k
Krasnyi Luch
Bălți
Kotovs'k
Voznesens'k
DNIPROPETROVS'K
DONETS'K
Makiïvka
MOLDOVA
Pivdennyy Buh
Kryvyi Rih
Zaporizhzhia
Novoshakhtinsk
Orhei
Nikopol
Mariupol'
Tiraspol
Mykolaïv
Melitopol
Berdians'k
Chișinău
Tighina
ODESA
Kherson
Dniapr
SEA OF AZOV
Cahul
Bilhorod-
Dnistrovs'kyi
Dzhankoi
Kiliya
Mys
Tarkhankut
CRIMEAN
PENINSULA
Kerch
Ievpatoriia
Simferopol'
Sevastopol'
Mys Sarych
Yalta

BLACK SEA

0   50   100   150   200   250   300 Miles
0   100   200   300   400   500 Kilometers

Scale 1:10,000,000; one inch to 158 miles
Copyright by Rand McNally & Co.
Made in U.S.A.
N-CMW50093-P1- -1-1-1

SOUTHEASTERN EUROPE

Except for Greece, Southeastern Europe was controlled by the Soviet Union for much of the 20th century. Since the Soviet Union broke apart in 1989-1991, the countries of Southeastern Europe have embraced their newfound freedom. However, some of them have also struggled to accommodate the many ethnic and religious differences that exist among their inhabitants. In Bosnia and Herzegovina, as well as in Yugoslavia, these tensions erupted into outright war. Today the region remains unstable, despite the diplomatic efforts of the United Nations and the international community.

Albanian refugees flee the fighting in Kosovo.

This castle in the Transylvania region of northwestern Romania inspired Dracula, *the famous story about a blood-sucking count.*

Some 2,500 years ago, the city-states of ancient Greece represented one of the most highly developed and influential civilizations the world has ever known. Today, Greece takes advantage of its lengthy sea coast to launch one of the world's largest merchant fleets, while its mild climate, impressive history, and lovely scenery make tourism an important part of the national economy.

The Karawanken Mountains rise behind an 11th century castle in Slovenia.

Whitewashed homes overlook the sea on the Greek island of Santorini.

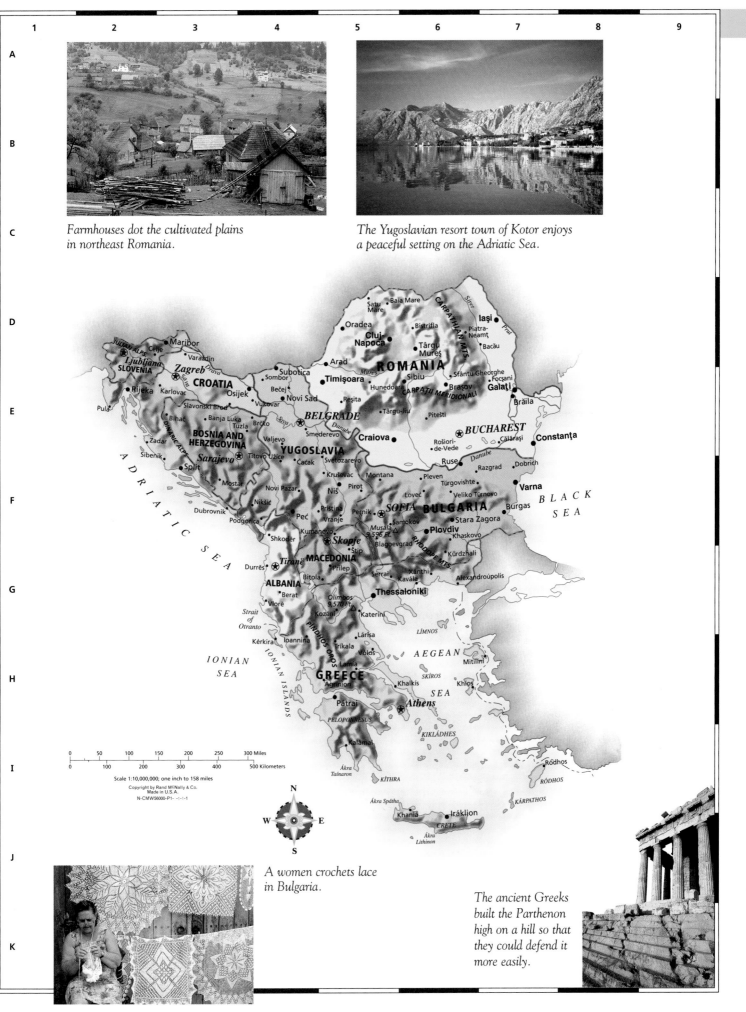

Farmhouses dot the cultivated plains in northeast Romania.

The Yugoslavian resort town of Kotor enjoys a peaceful setting on the Adriatic Sea.

A women crochets lace in Bulgaria.

The ancient Greeks built the Parthenon high on a hill so that they could defend it more easily.

AFRICA

Africa, the world's second-largest continent, is a land of dramatic and varied terrain. Narrow plains line the coast, while wide plateaus fill much of the continent's interior. Lush tropical rain forests flank the equator near the center of the continent. Sun-scorched deserts span the north and portions of the southwest, and grasslands called savannas lie between the deserts and the rain forests.

Across this vast continent are great rivers, mountains, and valleys. It contains four major rivers, but the Nile–the longest in the world–is the most important. It flows north across more than half of the continent before emptying into the Mediterranean Sea. Africa's mountain ranges include some majestic peaks such as Kilimanjaro in Tanzania. Between the mountain ranges of eastern Africa lies the Rift Valley, a long rip in the earth's surface that extends about 4,000 miles (almost 6,500 kilometers) and contains volcanoes, hot springs, and some of the world's largest and deepest lakes.

Egypt's ancient pyramids (above) have withstood the test of time; the African lion (left) is often called "King of Beasts"; Kilimanjaro (below) rises above the Amboseli Plain in Kenya.

Land Elevation
Feet (Meters)

- 9,840 and over (3,000 and over)
- 6,560 - 9,840 (2,000 - 3,000)
- 3,280 - 6,560 (1,000 - 2,000)
- 1,640 - 3,280 (500 - 1,000)
- 656 - 1,640 (200 - 500)
- 0 - 656 feet (0 - 200)

Scale 1:45,000,000; one inch to 710 miles

Copyright by Rand McNally & Co.
Made in U.S.A.
N-CMW80000-A1- -1-1-1

Africa Facts

Area: 11,700,000 square miles (30,300,000 square kilometers)

Highest Mountain: Kilimanjaro, Tanzania, 19,340 feet (5,895 meters)

Lowest Point: Lac Assal, Djibouti, -515 feet (-157 meters)

Longest River: Nile, 4,145 miles (6,671 kilometers) —*world's longest river*

Largest Lake: Lake Victoria, Kenya-Tanzania-Uganda, 26,820 square miles (69,463 square kilometers)

Largest Desert: Sahara, northern Africa, 3,500,000 square miles (9,065,000 square kilometers)—*world's largest desert*

Largest Island: Madagascar, 226,500 square miles (587,000 square kilometers)

THE LAND

The land in Africa offers up an assortment of riches–from gold and minerals found deep within the earth to the crops that grow at its surface. Different industries dominate different parts of the continent: Economic activity depends on the quality of the land and variations in regional climate. Many African countries depend on a single industry to drive the economy, but people in other areas are looking for new ways to make the most of their natural resources.

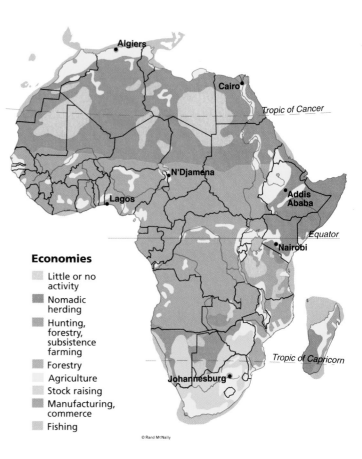

Economies

- Little or no activity
- Nomadic herding
- Hunting, forestry, subsistence farming
- Forestry
- Agriculture
- Stock raising
- Manufacturing, commerce
- Fishing

© Rand McNally

Economies

Most Africans are either farmers or herders. Many live as their ancestors did for thousands of years, continually moving across the land to follow animal herds, or living in small villages, raising crops and animals.

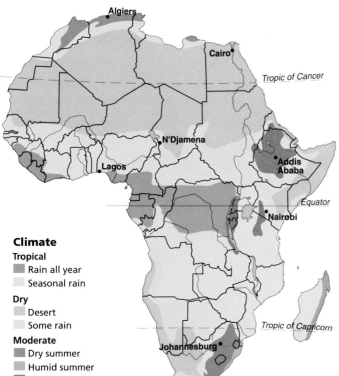

Climate

Tropical
- Rain all year
- Seasonal rain

Dry
- Desert
- Some rain

Moderate
- Dry summer
- Humid summer
- Rainy summer

Continental
- Long summer
- Short summer
- Very short, cool summer

Polar
- Tundra
- Ice cap

Highlands
- Varies with elevation

© Rand McNally

Climates

Africa is the world's hottest continent. One-third of Africa's land area is desert, but near the equator a tremendous amount of rain falls. The tropical rain forests of central Africa are hot and humid.

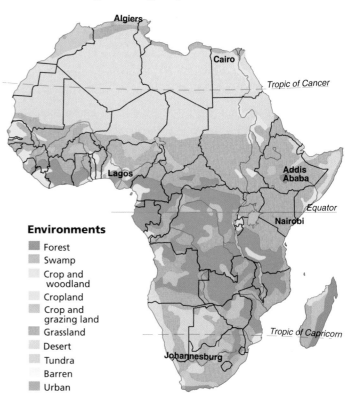

Environments

- Forest
- Swamp
- Crop and woodland
- Cropland
- Crop and grazing land
- Grassland
- Desert
- Tundra
- Barren
- Urban

© Rand McNally

Mining

Africa has some of the largest mineral reserves in the world, most of them untapped. The world's largest uranium mine is in Namibia, and copper is Zambia's major export. There are extensive oil fields in the forbidding deserts of northern Africa, and large gold, platinum, and diamond mines in South Africa.

World Gold Production

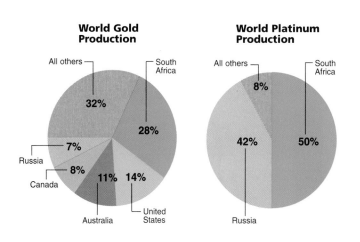

- All others 32%
- South Africa 28%
- Russia 7%
- Canada 8%
- Australia 11%
- United States 14%

World Platinum Production

- All others 8%
- South Africa 50%
- Russia 42%

This open-air bazaar in Algeria is a thriving marketplace.

Farming

Three out of four Africans work in agriculture. There are two major types of farming in Africa. The first is subsistence farming, when people grow enough food to feed themselves and their families. The second is commercial farming, when major companies grow large quantities of crops for sale. Commercial farms throughout central and southern Africa produce crops such as coffee, bananas, tobacco, and cocoa. Some of these items are sold only in African markets. Other yields, called cash crops, are grown specifically for canning, freezing, or refining, and are sold overseas.

Africa possesses approximately 40 percent of the world's hydroelectric potential. Kenya's Lake Kariba Dam provides power for the surrounding region.

Johannesburg is a prosperous South African city.

Tourism

Tourism is a major industry for many African countries that are not industrialized. Every year, hundreds of thousands of people flock to the deserts of Egypt to see the colossal pyramids and the mighty Sphinx, built thousands of years ago. The wildlife preserves in Kenya and Tanzania attract thousands of people from around the world who come to see and photograph the magnificent wildlife that lives there.

The Great Sphinx of Egypt is one of Africa's most-hallowed tourist destinations.

THE PEOPLE

Africa's more than 50 countries represent a complex mixture of peoples and cultures, with hundreds of ethnic groups and at least 1,000 different languages. For thousands of years, Africans organized themselves into tribal nations. From the 1600s into the 1960s, Europeans colonized most of the continent, but today the colonies are gone and nearly every country is independent. Although civil war has torn apart many of these countries, and Africa's population continues to face great challenges, the continent remains a place of opportunity due to the diversity of its cultures and resourcefulness of its people.

Schoolchildren wave the flag of South Africa on the steps of Parliament.

Masai women from Kenya wear colorful, traditional native dress.

In Burundi, men form a ceremonial circle to play tambor drums.

A young woman walks among a herd of camels in Morocco.

Africans travel and transport goods by camel because the animals are well adapted to desert life.

A little girl stands in front of a restaurant in a small town in Namibia.

The Arabian sitar is a popular musical instrument in northern Africa.

MEDITERRANEAN SEA

Strait of Gibraltar
ALGIERS
Rabat
CASABLANCA
MOROCCO
Marrakech
Wahran
Qacentina
Tunis
TUNISIA
Ghardaïa
Tripoli
Gulf of Sidra
Banghāzi
ALEXANDRIA
CAIRO
Suez
Asyūt

WESTERN SAHARA
ALGERIA
LIBYA
EGYPT
Tropic of Cancer
Aswān
Lake Nasser

El Aaiún

CAPE VERDE

MAURITANIA
MALI
NIGER
CHAD
SUDAN
Omdurman
Khartoum
ERITREA
Asmera
Port Sudan
RED SEA
Nile

Nouakchott
Timbuktu
Senegal
DAKAR
SENEGAL
THE GAMBIA
Bamako
Niger
Niamey
BURKINA FASO
Ouagadougou
Lake Chad
N'Djamena
Kano
NIGERIA
Abuja
Benue
Chari
CENTRAL AFRICAN REPUBLIC
Bangui
Bomu
DJIBOUTI
Djibouti
Lake Tana
Blue Nile
ADDIS ABABA
SOMALIA
ETHIOPIA
Gulf of Aden
Mountain Nile
Shabelle
Wabe

GUINEA-BISSAU
GUINEA
Conakry
Freetown
SIERRA LEONE
Monrovia
LIBERIA
COTE D'IVOIRE
GHANA
BENIN
TOGO
Volta Lake
Cotonou
LAGOS
Accra
ABIDJAN
CAMEROON
DOUALA
Yaoundé
EQUATORIAL GUINEA
SAO TOME AND PRINCIPE
Libreville
GABON
CONGO
Congo
Ubangi
Kisangani
DEM. REP. OF THE CONGO
Uele
UGANDA
Lake Rudolf
Mogadishu
Equator
Mogadishu

ATLANTIC OCEAN

Brazzaville
KINSHASA
Kasai
Cuango
LUANDA
Cuanza
RWANDA
Kigali
Bujumbura
BURUNDI
Kampala
Lake Victoria
KENYA
NAIROBI
Mombasa
INDIAN OCEAN
SEYCHELLES

ANGOLA
Lobito
Huambo
Lualaba
Lubumbashi
Mbuji-Mayi
Lake Tanganyika
TANZANIA
Dodoma
DAR ES SALAAM

N
W E
S

COMOROS
MALAWI
Lake Nyasa
ZAMBIA
Lusaka
Ndola
Lilongwe
MAYOTTE (Fr.)
Lake Kariba
Zambezi
Okavango
Cunene
Harare
ZIMBABWE
MOZAMBIQUE
Beira
Mozambique Channel
ANTANANARIVO
MADAGASCAR
MAURITIUS
REUNION (Fr.)
Tropic of Capricorn

NAMIBIA
Windhoek
BOTSWANA
Gaborone
Limpopo
Changane
Pretoria
Johannesburg
MAPUTO
SWAZILAND
LESOTHO
Maseru
Durban

SOUTH AFRICA
Orange
Cape Town
Port Elizabeth

Africa Facts

Population:
770,300,000

Population Density:
66 people per square mile
(25 per square kilometer)

Most Populous Country:
Nigeria, 112,170,000 people

Largest City:
Cairo, Egypt, 13,250,000 people
(metropolitan area)

0 200 400 600 800 1000 Miles
0 300 600 900 1200 1500 Kilometers

Scale 1:45,000,000; one inch to 710 miles

NORTHERN AFRICA

N
W E
S

Strait of Gibraltar

ALGIERS • Tizi-Ouzou • Skikda • Annaba
Ceuta (Sp.) • Wahran • Mestghanem • Stif • Qacentina • Tunis
Tanger • Tétouan • Melilla (Sp.) • Bou Saâda • Batna • Tbessa • Sousse • Mona
Al Hoceima • Sidi bel Abbès • Khenchla • Kairouan
Salé • Oujda • Tilimsen • Beskra • Sfax
Rabat • Fès • ATLAS • Gabès
CASABLANCA • Meknes • Laghouat • Touggourt • TUNISIA • Ra
Khenifra • MOUNTAINS • Az Zâw
Settat • Beni-Mellal • Ghardaïa • Wargla • Tri
Safi
Marrakech • Béchar
Essaouira
MOROCCO • GRAND ERG OCCIDENTAL
Cap Rhir • Ouarzazate • GRAND ERG ORIENTAL
Jebel Toubkal • A L G E R I A
Agadir • 13,665 Ft. • TRIPO
Oued Drâa • S A H A R
El Aaiún
Smara
Cabo Boujdour • 'ERG IGUIDI
WESTERN • Ghât
SAHARA • EL HANK • 'ERG CHECH
Tropic of Cancer • Dakhla • Tahat • 9,541 Ft. • F
Cap Barbas • Fdérik • OUARÂNE • IJÂFENE • AHAGGAR
Nouâdhibou • Gréboun • 6,378 Ft.
Ràs Nouâdhibou • ADRAR • A Ï R
Ràs Timirist • MAURITANIA • DES • Idoûkâl-en-Taghès
IFÔGHAS • 6,634 Ft.
Nouakchott • MALI • N I G E R
CAPE VERDE • Timbuktu • Niger • Gao • SU
SANTO • *Sénégal* • Doro
ANTÃO • Saint-Louis • Kaédi • Hombori Tondo • Tahoua
SÃO NICOLAU • BOA VISTA • Louga • 3,789 Ft.
FOGO • MAO • Thiès • Mopti • Maradi • Zinder
Praia • DAKAR • Kaolack • Ségou • Niamey • Sokoto • Nguru • Gashu
SANTIAGO • SENEGAL • Kayes • BURKINA FASO • Birnin Kebbi • Katsina • Hadejia
Banjul • Tambacounda • Bamako • Koutiala • Ouagadougou • Jega • Gusau • Azare • Maidu
THE GAMBIA • *Cambie* • Sikasso • Koudougou • Zaria • Kano • Potiskum
Ziguinchor • Bobo Dioulasso • Kaduna • Bauchi • Gombe
Bissau • Labé • GUINEA • Kankan • BENIN • Minna • Jos • Bénué
GUINEA-BISSAU • *Niger* • Korhogo • Parakou • Lafiagi • Abuja • NIGERIA
Conakry • Makeni • Beyla • Tamale • Sokodé • Keffi • JOS PLATEAU • Makurdi
SIERRA LEONE • Bo • COTE D'IVOIRE • Volta Lake • Iseyin • Ogbomosho • Lokoja • Gboko
Freetown • Kenema • Koindu • Nzerekoré • Bouaké • GHANA • TOGO • Ibadan • Oshogbo • Enugu
Mt. Nimba • Man • Yamoussoukro • Kumasi • Abeokuta • Benin • Onitsha • Bamenda • ADAMA
5,748 Ft. • Daloa • Abengourou • Cotonou • LAGOS • City • Foumban
Monrovia • Gagnoa • Agboville • Lomé • Porto-Novo • Sapele • Aba • Calabar • CAMER
Buchanan • Accra • Port Harcourt • Nkongsamba
LIBERIA • San-Pédro • Cape Coast • Nembe • Kûmba • DOUALA
ABIDJAN • Winneba • BIOKO • Malabo • Edéa • Yao
Growa Point • Sekondi-Takoradi
Gulf of Guinea
EQUATORIAL
GUINEA
A T L A N T I C   O C E A N
SAO TOME
AND PRINCIPE
Equator
ANNOBÓN

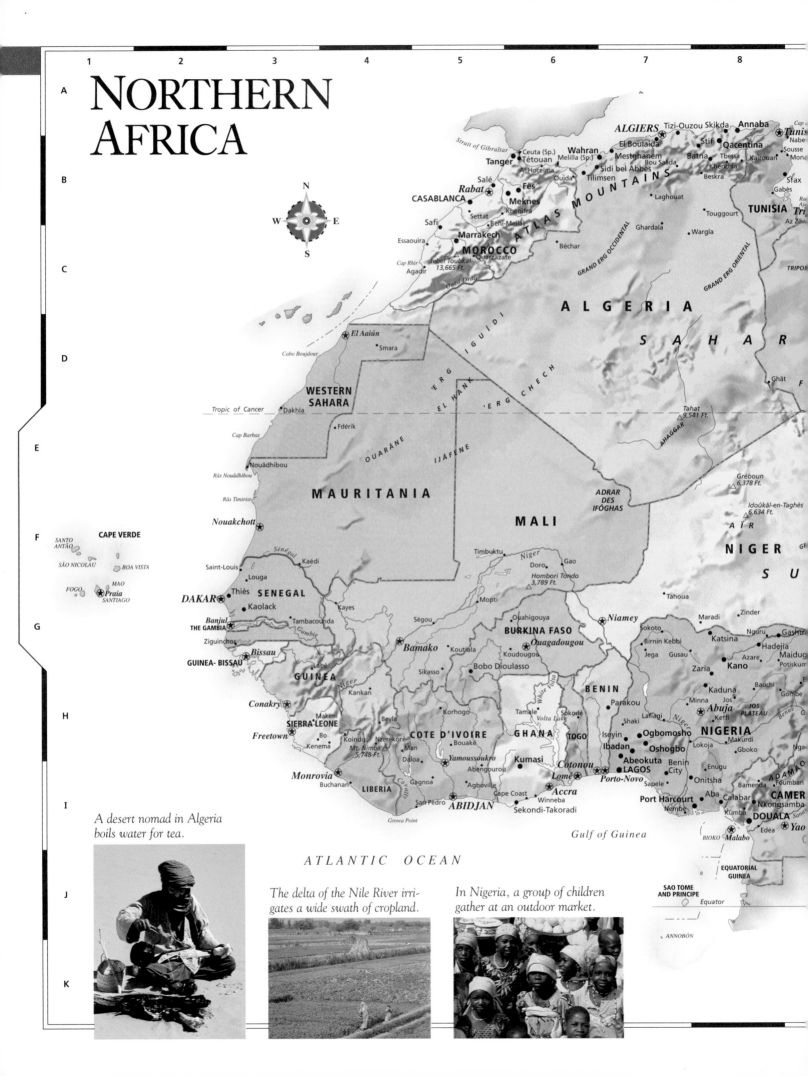

A desert nomad in Algeria
boils water for tea.

The delta of the Nile River irri-
gates a wide swath of cropland.

In Nigeria, a group of children
gather at an outdoor market.

10   11   12   13   14   15   16   17

Most of Northern Africa is dry, barren desert. The Sahara––the largest desert in the world––spreads across more than half of the region. Algeria and Libya are almost entirely covered by desert. Most of the people who live in this harsh environment are nomads. They travel from place to place with their herds of goats, sheep, and camels in search of water and grazing pastures. The southern Sahara gives way to the Sahel, a wide band of dry grasslands. Some crops grow there, but overfarming is causing the land to lose soil and become desert. The valleys of the Atlas Mountains offer some fertile land, but most of the richest land in Northern Africa is found to the east, in the Nile River Valley. People have farmed this fruitful land for more than 7,000 years. Farther south, the Sahel yields to the steamy tropical rain forests of central Africa. Even though the region is ripe for farming, and oil reserves have been discovered in the area around the Gulf of Guinea, most of the people still struggle with poverty.

MEDITERRANEAN SEA

Misrātah
Banghāzi
Al Baydā'
Darnah
Tubruq
Gulf of Sidra

CYRENAICA

ALEXANDRIA   Port Said
Tanta   **El Mansûra**
QATTARA DEPRESSION   Ismailia
CAIRO   Suez
El Fayoum   Giza
Beni Suef
Maghâgha   Beni Mazâr
El Minya   *SINAI PEN.*
Mallawi
Manfalût   Asyût
Tahta   Suhag
Girga   Qena
Luxor
Isna
Kom Ombo
Aswân

L I B Y A
WESTERN DESERT
EGYPT
• Al Jawf

ARABIAN DESERT
Nile

LIBYAN DESERT

Bikkū Bitti △ 7,438 Ft.
Pic Toussside △ 10,876 Ft.

Lake Nasser
Râs Banâs

Tropic of Cancer

RED SEA

Ra's al Hadâribah

NUBIAN DESERT

T I B E S T I
Emi Koussi 11,204 Ft.

Ra's Kasr

Port Sudan

ENNEDI

'Aṭbarah

Nile

ERITREA
Akordat   Keren   Mitsiwa

N   CHAD

Omdurman   Al Kharṭām Baḥrī
✪ **Khartoum**   Kassalâ
Asmera
Chad
Abéché   Al Fāshir
Al Junaynah   **S U D A N**   Wad Madanī
Mekele   Aseb
Nyala   Al Qaḍârif   △ Ras Dashen
An Nuhūd   Sannâr   *Terara 15,158 Ft.*   *DENAKIL*
Al Ubayyid   Gonder
S A H E L   Ad Duwaym   *Lake Tana*   **DJIBOUTI**
✪ **N'Djamena**   Bahir Dar   Dese   ✪ *Djibouti*   *Gulf of Aden*
Kelo   *White Nile*   Talo   *ETHIOPIAN*   Ra's Khaanziir   *Gees Gwardo*
Birao   *Blue Nile*   △ 14,478 Ft.   Berbera   Boosaaso
Moundou   Debre Markos   *PLATEAU*   Dire   Hargeysa
Khazzân ar   Dawa
Chari   Ruṣayris   **E T H I O P I A**   Harer
Sarh   Malakâl   ✪ *ADDIS ABABA*   *SOMALIA*
Mountain Nile   Debre   *OGADEN*
MASSIF DES BONGO   Zeyit
Asela
Waw   *A S   S U D D*   Jima   Dhuusa
Mareeb
CENTRAL AFRICAN REPUBLIC   *Lake Abaya*   *RIFT VALLEY*   *Shebele*
Bambari   *Guge 13,780 Ft.*   *Genale*
Mambere   Juba
✪ *Bangui*   *Oubangui*   *Shebele*   *INDIAN OCEAN*
Mbomou
Baidoa

✪ *Mogadishu*

Shabeelle

0   100   200   300   400   500   600 Miles
0   200   400   600   800   1000 Kilometers

Equator
Scale 1:20,000,000; one inch to 315 miles
Kismaayo

Raas Jumbo

SOUTHERN AFRICA

Like the land to the north, Southern Africa is known for a number of outstanding natural features. In the eastern part of the region, the Rift Valley, a great gash in the earth's surface, stretches about 4,000 miles (almost 6,500 kilometers) from Ethiopia south to Zambia.

Cheetah

Mountain ranges rise along both sides of the Valley. In the surrounding savannas, or grasslands, large herds of zebras, elephants, rhinoceroses, giraffes, wildebeests, and other animals roam the land. South of the grasslands are the Kalahari and Namib Deserts. Most people in Southern Africa live in small villages, but the region also contains the major cities of Nairobi, Kenya, and Kinshasa, Democratic Republic of the Congo.

In Tanzania's Serengeti National Park, acacia trees rise up from the grasslands.

African animals come in all sizes and shapes:

Fennec Fox   *Bongo*   *African Elephant*

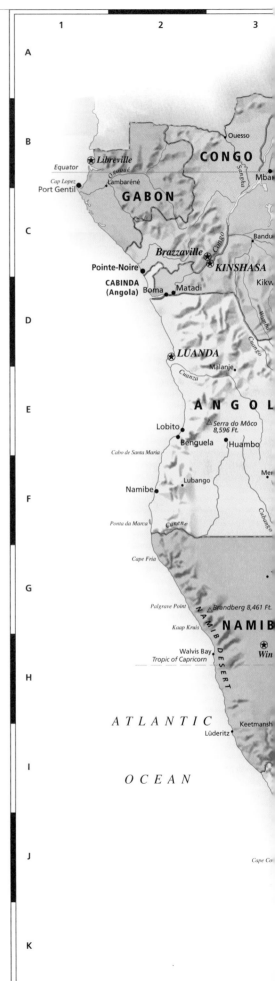

Ouesso

CONGO

Equator

Libreville

Oguoué

Cap Lopez
Port Gentil
Lambaréné

GABON

Mba

Congo

Sangha

Bandu

Brazzaville   Congo

Pointe-Noire   KINSHASA

CABINDA
(Angola)   Boma   Matadi

Kikw

Wamba

LUANDA
Malanje

Cuanza

Cuango

Cuanza

Cuango

ANGOL

Lobito   Serra do Môco
8,596 Ft.

Benguela   Huambo

Cabo de Santa Maria

Me

Namibe   Lubango

Ponta da Marca   Cunene

Cubango

Cape Fria

Brandberg 8,461 Ft.

Palgrave Point

NAMIB

Kaap Kruis   NAMIB

Walvis Bay
Tropic of Capricorn   DESERT   Win

ATLANTIC

Keetmansh

Lüderitz

OCEAN

Cape Co

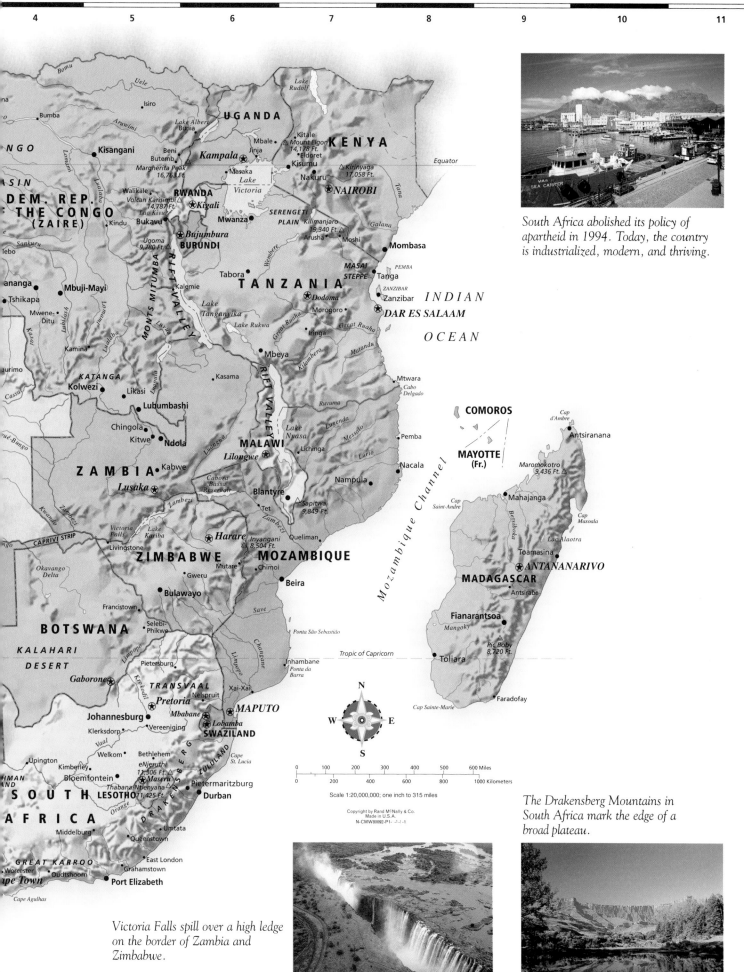

South Africa abolished its policy of apartheid in 1994. Today, the country is industrialized, modern, and thriving.

The Drakensberg Mountains in South Africa mark the edge of a broad plateau.

Victoria Falls spill over a high ledge on the border of Zambia and Zimbabwe.

ASIA

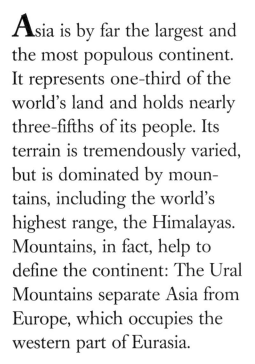

Asia is by far the largest and the most populous continent. It represents one-third of the world's land and holds nearly three-fifths of its people. Its terrain is tremendously varied, but is dominated by mountains, including the world's highest range, the Himalayas. Mountains, in fact, help to define the continent: The Ural Mountains separate Asia from Europe, which occupies the western part of Eurasia.

Asia is notable for its extremes. Mount Everest, on the Nepal-China border, is the world's highest mountain. The Tibetan Plateau is the world's largest and highest plateau. The shore of the salty Dead Sea, which lies between Israel and Jordan, is the lowest point on Earth. Lake Baikal in Siberia is the world's deepest lake.

India's Taj Mahal (above) was built to honor an emperor's wife; Japanese fans (left) are ornate works of art; the Great Wall of China (below) is the largest man-made structure in the world

ARCTIC OCEAN

SEVERNAYA
ZEMLYA

NEW SIBERIAN
ISLANDS

EAST SIBERIAN
SEA

LAPTEV
SEA

KARA SEA

BERING
SEA

pol.
Yamal

poluostrov
Taymyr

Noril'sk

Central

Siberian

Uplands

Arctic Circle

Kolyma

poluostrov
Kamchatka

Ural Mountains

West

Siberian

Lowland

Ob'

RUSSIA

Lena

Verkhoyanskiy khrebet

Mts Lopatka

SEA OF
OKHOTSK

Yenisey

S i b e r i a

NOVOSIBIRSK

Irtysh

Ishim

Angara

Lake
Baikal

Stanovoy khrebet

SAKHALIN

Tatar
Strait

KURIL ISLANDS

Kirghiz
Steppe

Aral
Sea

Sayan Mts.

Altai

Selenge

Greater Khingan Range

Manchuria

Sikhote-Alin

SEA OF
JAPAN

HOKKAIDO

KAZAKHSTAN

Ust-Urt
Plateau

Ural

Lake
Balkhash

Syr Darya

Junggar Pendi

MONGOLIA

Gobi

BEIJING ✪

HONSHŪ

JAPAN

TŌKYŌ

TURKMENISTAN

UZBEKISTAN

KYRGYZSTAN

Amu Darya

Tien Shan

NORTH
KOREA

SOUTH
KOREA

Mt. Fuji △
12,388 Ft.

SHIKOKU

KYŪSHŪ

Korea Strait

TAJIKISTAN

Pamir

Tarim Pendi

Qilian Shan

YELLOW
SEA

PACIFIC
OCEAN

Hindu Kush

K2
28,250 Ft.

Altun Shan

Qaidam
Pendi

AFGHANISTAN

Kunlun Shan

CHINA

Qin Ling

Huang

EAST

Plateau of Tibet

SHANGHAI

CHINA SEA

PAKISTAN

New
Delhi ✪

NEPAL

Mt. Everest △
29,028 Ft.

Himalayas

BHUTAN

Nan Ling

Wuyi Shan

Tropic of Cancer

Indus

Ganges

Brahmaputra

Yangtze

Taiwan Strait

TAIWAN

Great
Indian
Desert

BANGLADESH

Gulf of
Oman

INDIA

Godavari

Deccan

Western Ghats

Eastern Ghats

MYANMAR

LAOS

Indochina

Red

Gulf of
Tonkin

Luzon Strait

HAINAN DAO

LUZON

Manila

PHILIPPINES

MUMBAI
(BOMBAY)

ARABIAN
SEA

Kāthiāwār
Peninsula

Irrawaddy

Mekong

THAILAND

BANGKOK ✪

CAMBODIA

VIETNAM

SOUTH CHINA
SEA

MINDANAO

LAKSHADWEEP

Cape Comorin

SRI LANKA

Bay of
Bengal

ANDAMAN
ISLANDS

Gulf of
Thailand

Sulu Sea

Celebes Sea

MALDIVES

Andaman
Sea

Mui Ca Mau

MOLUCCAS

NICOBAR
ISLANDS

Malay
Peninsula

BRUNEI

CELEBES

CERAM

NEW
GUINEA

Equator

Str. of Malacca

MALAYSIA

SINGAPORE ✪

BORNEO

Banda Sea

Arafura Sea

SUMATRA

GREATER SUNDA ISLANDS

Java Sea

INDONESIA

TIMOR

INDIAN OCEAN

Equator

Jakarta ✪

JAVA

Timor Sea

Asia Facts

Area: 17,300,000 square miles
(44,900,000 square kilometers)

Highest Mountain:
Mount Everest, China-Nepal,
29,028 feet (8,848 meters)—
world's highest mountain

Lowest Point: Dead Sea,
Israel-Jordan, -1339 feet
(-408 meters)—*world's
lowest point*

Longest River: Yangtze, China,
3,900 miles (6,300 kilometers)

Largest Lake: Caspian Sea
Asia/Europe, 143,240 square
miles (370,990 square
kilometers)

Largest Desert: Gobi, Mongo-
lia-China, 500,000 square miles
(1,295,000 square kilometers)

Largest Island: New Guinea
Asia/Oceania,
309,000 square miles
(800,000 square kilometers)

Land Elevation
Feet (Meters)

9,840 and over (3,000 and over)

6,560 - 9,840 (2,000 - 3,000)

3,280 - 6,560 (1,000 - 2,000)

1,640 - 3,280 (500 - 1,000)

656 - 1,640 (200 - 500)

0 - 656 feet (0 - 200)

0   100   300   500 Miles
0   200   400   600   800 Kilometers
Scale 1:45,000,000; one inch to 710 miles

N
W   E
S

THE LAND

Only about a fifth of the continent is suitable for agriculture, but a large portion of Asia's people make their living off the land. In Asia's three most populous countries–China, India, and Russia–two-thirds of workers are farmers. Raising livestock is also an important job, especially in the central Asian grasslands. Given Asia's size, it is not surprising that the continent holds some of the world's largest reserves of oil, natural gas, and coal.

By building terraces that capture rainfall, farmers can grow rice on even the steepest hillsides.

Environments

Asia has a wide variety of environments, including large areas of arctic and subarctic tundra, broad deserts, heavy forests, and dry grasslands.

Environments

- Forest
- Swamp
- Crop and woodland
- Cropland
- Crop and grazing land
- Grassland
- Desert
- Tundra
- Barren
- Urban

Wood products are one of Indonesia's main exports.

Arctic Circle

Tehran

Beijing

Tōkyō

Tropic of Cancer

Mumbai (Bombay)

Bangkok

Equator

Jakarta

© Rand McNally

Mineral Resources

In addition to its huge oil and coal reserves, Asia is also rich in metals such as iron ore, tin, lead, zinc, and bauxite. The continent furnishes raw materials for its own industries with plenty left over to export to the rest of the world.

Farming

Rice is Asia's most important crop: Asia produces 90 percent of the world's supply. Rice grows both in flooded fields called paddies and on terraced hillsides. With plentiful rainfall and fertile lowlands, countries such as India, Thailand, and China are the perfect places to grow rice–in fact, some areas grow three separate rice crops each year.

Forestry

In chilly Siberia, forests cover more than one-third of the land. In southeast Asia, the exotic hardwoods in the rain forests are used mainly for making furniture. Unfortunately, the trees are being cut down faster than they can grow back, and entire Asian forests are in danger of disappearing.

Tourism

Tourism is an important source of income for many Asian countries. The continent offers a broad range of travel destinations, including the Taj Mahal, China's Great Wall, Mount Everest and other high Himalayan peaks, the ancient temples of Myanmar, and holy sites of the Middle East.

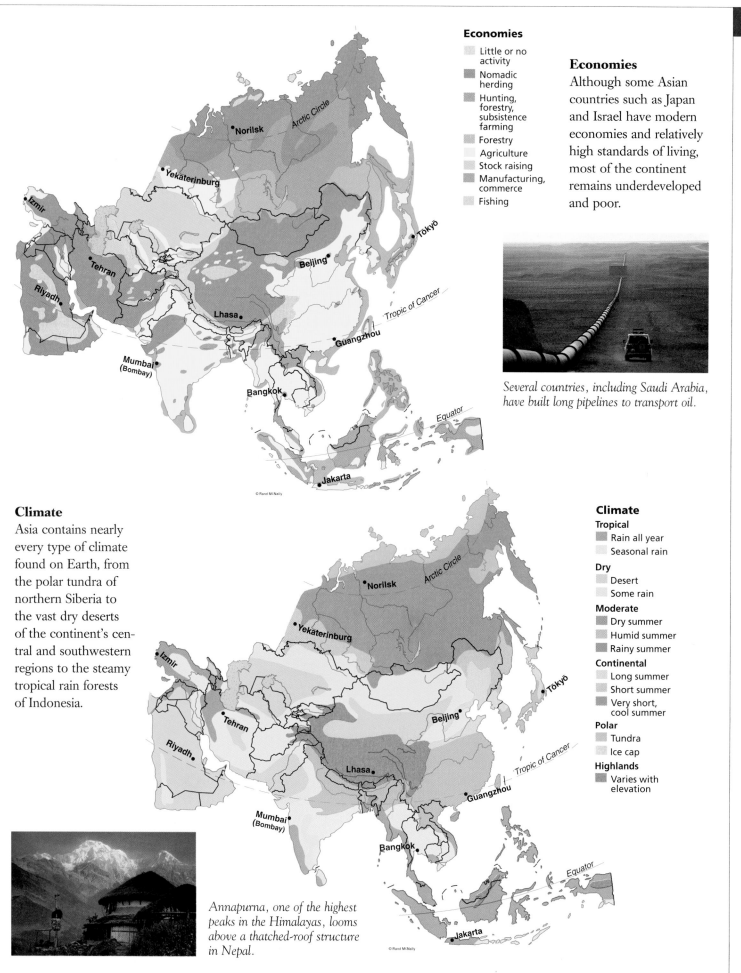

Economies

Little or no activity

Nomadic herding

Hunting, forestry, subsistence farming

Forestry

Agriculture

Stock raising

Manufacturing, commerce

Fishing

Economies

Although some Asian countries such as Japan and Israel have modern economies and relatively high standards of living, most of the continent remains underdeveloped and poor.

Several countries, including Saudi Arabia, have built long pipelines to transport oil.

Climate

Asia contains nearly every type of climate found on Earth, from the polar tundra of northern Siberia to the vast dry deserts of the continent's central and southwestern regions to the steamy tropical rain forests of Indonesia.

Climate

Tropical

Rain all year

Seasonal rain

Dry

Desert

Some rain

Moderate

Dry summer

Humid summer

Rainy summer

Continental

Long summer

Short summer

Very short, cool summer

Polar

Tundra

Ice cap

Highlands

Varies with elevation

Annapurna, one of the highest peaks in the Himalayas, looms above a thatched-roof structure in Nepal.

THE PEOPLE

Asia is the most culturally and ethnically diverse continent, mainly due to its enormous size. Three out of every five people on Earth live in Asia. While many Asians are farmers and live in the countryside or in small villages, the continent's cities are among the world's largest and most crowded. Tokyo, Japan, is the most populous metropolitan area on Earth. China, with more than one billion people, is the world's most populous country.

Sleds drawn by reindeer help Siberians travel across the deep snow.

Chinese children perform at a festival.

In India, a merchant keeps track of business transactions in a ledger.

As part of their Islamic faith, Muslims observe the holy month of Ramadan.

Buddhist monks gather outside a temple in Bangkok, Thailand.

A young herder tends sheep and cattle in the mountains of Uzbekistan.

Asia Facts

Population: 3,629,100,000

Population Density:
210 per square mile
(81 per square kilometer)

Most Populous Country:
China, 1,242,070,000 people

Largest City:
Tokyo-Yokohama, Japan,
31,500,000 people
(metropolitan area)

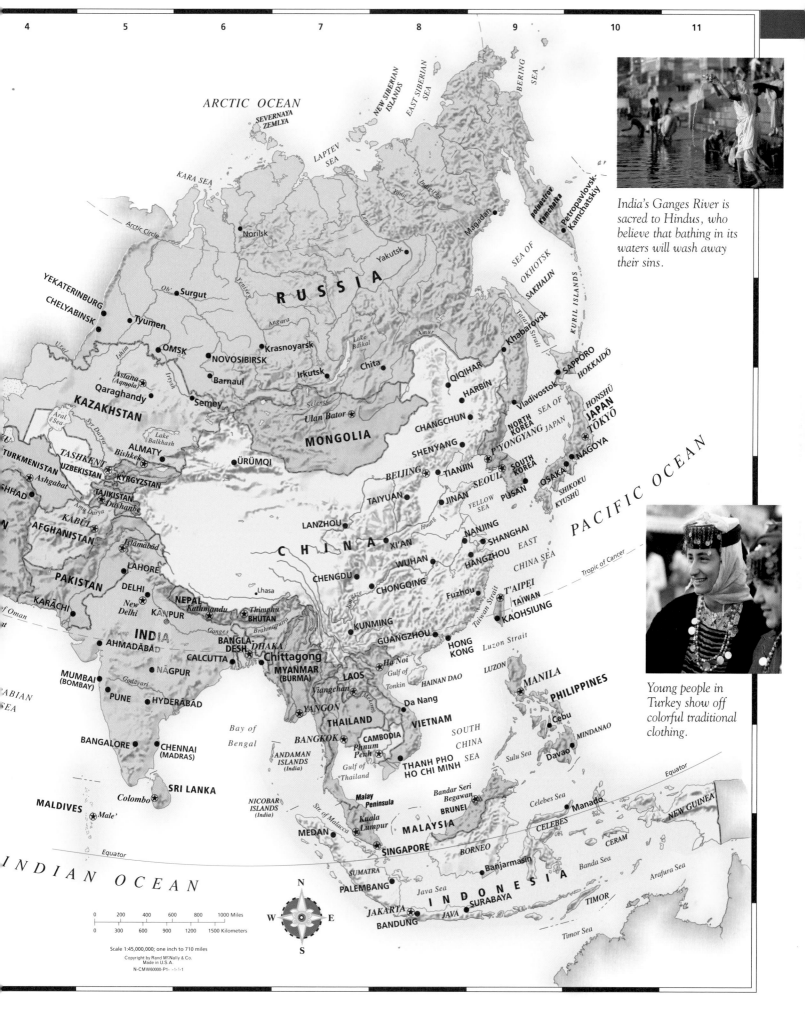

4   5   6   7   8   9   10   11

ARCTIC OCEAN

SEVERNAYA
ZEMLYA

NEW SIBERIAN
ISLANDS

EAST SIBERIAN
SEA

LAPTEV
SEA

KARA SEA

BERING
SEA

Arctic Circle

Norilsk

• Surgut
Ob'
Yenisey

Yakutsk •

Magadan

Poluostrov
Kamchatka

Petropavlovsk-
Kamchatskiy

YEKATERINBURG

CHELYABINSK

R U S S I A

SEA OF
OKHOTSK

Tyumen •

Angara

Amur

Khabarovsk

SAKHALIN

KURIL ISLANDS

OMSK •

Krasnoyarsk •

Lake
Baikal

Chita •

QIQIHAR •

SAPPORO

HOKKAIDŌ

Irtysh

NOVOSIBIRSK •

Irkutsk •

HARBIN •

Vladivostok •

HONSHŪ

Astana
(Aqmola) ✳

Barnaul •

Selenge

CHANGCHUN •

NORTH
KOREA
P'YONGYANG ✳

SEA OF
JAPAN

JAPAN

TŌKYŌ

Qaraghandy •

Semey •

Ulan Bator ✳

KAZAKHSTAN

SHENYANG •

Syr Darya

Aral
Sea

Lake
Balkhash

MONGOLIA

SOUTH
KOREA

OSAKA

NAGOYA

SHIKOKU

ALMATY •

BEIJING •

TIANJIN •

SEOUL ✳

KYŪSHŪ

TASHKENT ✳

Bishkek ✳

ÜRÜMQI •

PUSAN •

TURKMENISTAN

UZBEKISTAN

KYRGYZSTAN

TAIYUAN •

JINAN •

YELLOW
SEA

Ashgabat ✳

Amy Darya

TAJIKISTAN

Dushanbe ✳

LANZHOU •

Huang

NANJING •

SHANGHAI •

MESHHAD

KABUL ✳

C H I N A

XI'AN •

HANGZHOU •

EAST
CHINA SEA

PACIFIC OCEAN

AFGHANISTAN

Tropic of Cancer

Islamabad ✳

WUHAN •

CHONGQING •

CHENGDU •

Yangtze

PAKISTAN

LAHORE •

Fuzhou •

T'AIPEI •

TAIWAN

DELHI •

Lhasa •

KUNMING •

KAOHSIUNG •

KARĀCHI •

New
Delhi ✳

KĀNPUR •

NEPAL

Kathmandu ✳

Brahmaputra

Thimphu ✳

BHUTAN

GUANGZHOU •

HONG
KONG

Luzon Strait

Gulf of
Oman

AHMADĀBĀD •

INDIA

Ganges

BANGLA-
DESH

DHAKA •

Chittagong •

Ho Noi •

LUZON

Taiwan Strait

CALCUTTA •

MYANMAR
(BURMA)

LAOS

HAINAN DAO

NĀGPUR •

Gulf of
Tonkin

MUMBAI
(BOMBAY) •

Godavari

Viangchan ✳

Da Nang •

MANILA ✳

PHILIPPINES

Cebu •

ARABIAN
SEA

PUNE •

HYDERĀBĀD •

YANGON ✳

THAILAND

VIETNAM

SOUTH

MINDANAO

BANGALORE •

CHENNAI
(MADRAS) •

BANGKOK ✳

CAMBODIA

CHINA

Davao •

Phnum
Penh ✳

SEA

ANDAMAN
ISLANDS
(India)

Gulf of
Thailand

THANH PHO
HO CHI MINH

Sulu Sea

SRI LANKA

Bay of
Bengal

Bandar Seri
Begawan ✳

Celebes Sea

Manado •

Colombo •

NICOBAR
ISLANDS
(India)

Str. of Malacca

Equator

MALDIVES

Male' ✳

Malay
Peninsula

BRUNEI

NEW GUINEA

Kuala
Lumpur ✳

MALAYSIA

CELEBES

CERAM

MEDAN •

BORNEO

INDIAN OCEAN

SINGAPORE ✳

Banjarmasin •

Banda Sea

Arafura Sea

SUMATRA

Java Sea

I N D O N E S I A

TIMOR

PALEMBANG •

SURABAYA •

JAKARTA ✳

JAVA

Timor Sea

BANDUNG •

0   200   400   600   800   1000 Miles

0   300   600   900   1200   1500 Kilometers

N
W — E
S

Scale 1:45,000,000; one inch to 710 miles
Copyright by Rand McNally & Co.
Made in U.S.A.
N-CMW60000-P1- -1-1-1

India's Ganges River is
sacred to Hindus, who
believe that bathing in its
waters will wash away
their sins.

Young people in
Turkey show off
colorful traditional
clothing.

SOUTHWEST ASIA

Southwest Asia borders Europe–in fact, a small part of Turkey actually falls within Europe. Turkey's most fertile farmlands spread along its lengthy coast, although wheat and barley grow in the dry plateau area in the center of the country. Armenia, Azerbaijan, and Georgia, which all lie in the mountainous region between the Black Sea and the Caspian Sea, possess abundant mineral wealth.

A Turkish farmer rides a donkey across a wheat field.

Grapes ripen on vines in the rugged Troodos Mountains, which dominate the center of the island of Cyprus.

Sheep graze near an ancient Roman temple in western Armenia.

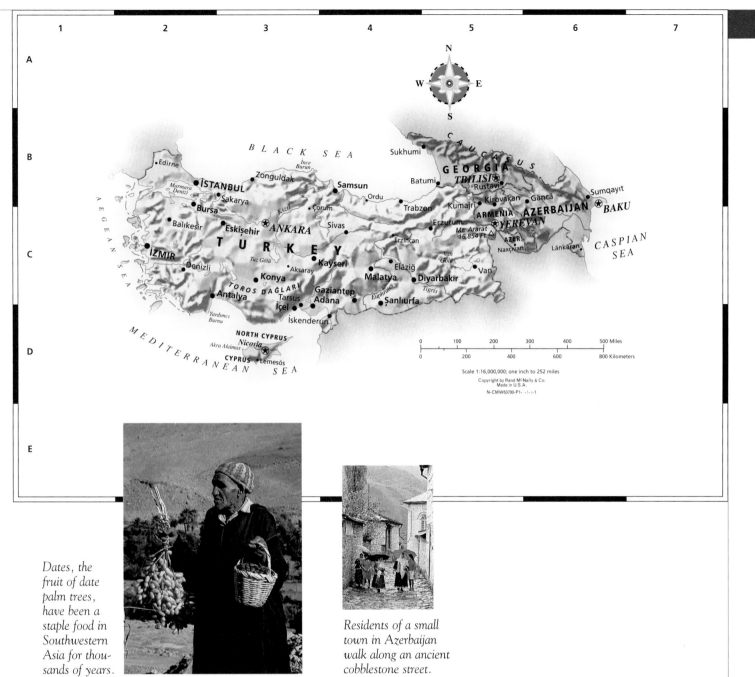

BLACK SEA

Edirne
Zonguldak
İnce Burun
Sukhumi
GEORGIA
Batumi
TBILISI
Rustavi
Sumqayıt
İSTANBUL
Marmara Denizi
Sakarya
Samsun
Ordu
Kumajri
Kirovakan
Gäncä
Bursa
Çorum
Trabzon
BAKU
Balıkesir
Eskişehir
Kızıl
Sivas
Erzurum
ARMENIA
AZERBAIJAN
ANKARA
Erzincan
Mt. Ararat 16,854 Ft.
YEREVAN
İZMIR
T U R K E Y
AZER.
Denizli
Tuz Gölü
Aksaray
Kayseri
Elâziğ
Van Gölü
Naxçıvan
Länkäran
CASPIAN SEA
Van
Konya
Malatya
Diyarbakır
TOROS DAĞLARI
Gaziantep
Tigris
Antalya
Tarsus
Adana
Euphrates
Şanlıurfa
İçel
Yardımcı Burnu
İskenderun
CAUCASUS
AEGEAN SEA
NORTH CYPRUS
Akra Akámas
Nicosia
CYPRUS
Lemesós
M E D I T E R R A N E A N   S E A

N W E S

0 100 200 300 400 500 Miles
0 200 400 600 800 Kilometers

Scale 1:16,000,000; one inch to 252 miles
Copyright by Rand McNally & Co.
Made in U.S.A.
N-CMW63700-P1- -1-:-1

Dates, the fruit of date palm trees, have been a staple food in Southwestern Asia for thousands of years.

Residents of a small town in Azerbaijan walk along an ancient cobblestone street.

Istanbul's magnificent Church of Hagia Sofia rises above the Bosporus Strait, which separates Asia and Europe.

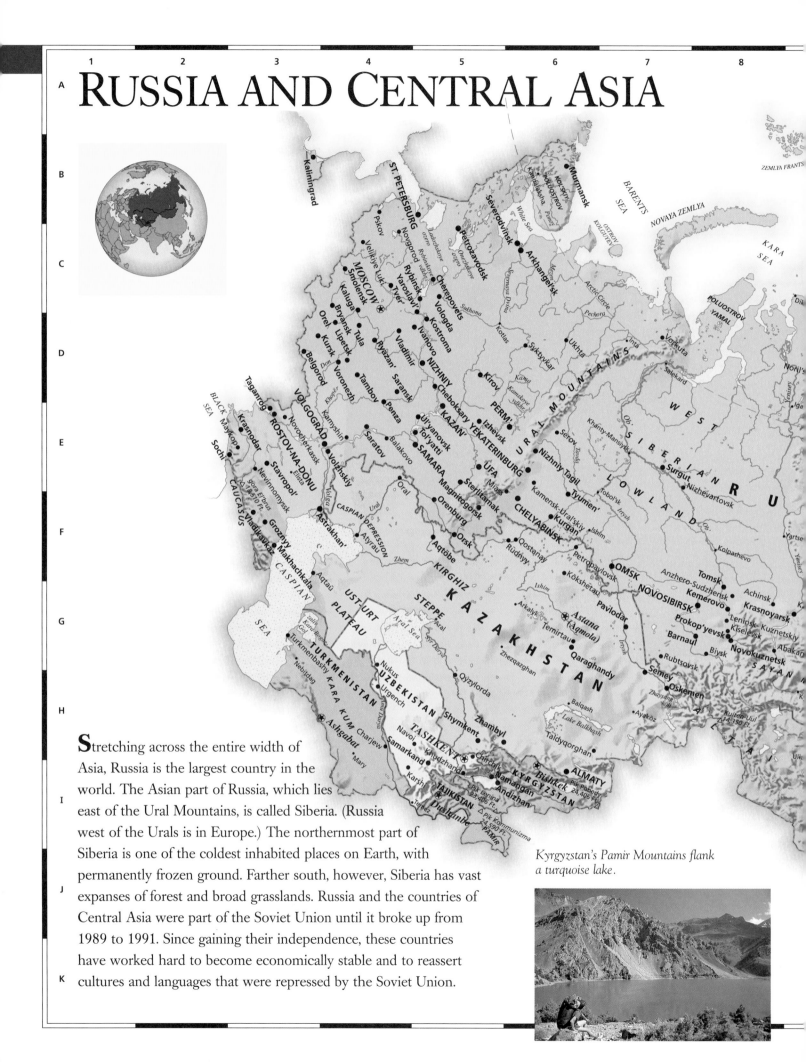

RUSSIA AND CENTRAL ASIA

Stretching across the entire width of Asia, Russia is the largest country in the world. The Asian part of Russia, which lies east of the Ural Mountains, is called Siberia. (Russia west of the Urals is in Europe.) The northernmost part of Siberia is one of the coldest inhabited places on Earth, with permanently frozen ground. Farther south, however, Siberia has vast expanses of forest and broad grasslands. Russia and the countries of Central Asia were part of the Soviet Union until it broke up from 1989 to 1991. Since gaining their independence, these countries have worked hard to become economically stable and to reassert cultures and languages that were repressed by the Soviet Union.

Kyrgyzstan's Pamir Mountains flank a turquoise lake.

10   11   12   13   14   15   16   17

N
W   E
S

C T I C   O C E A N

OSTROV KOMSOMOLETS
SEVERNAYA ZEMLYA

OSTROV
BOL'SHEVIK

NEW SIBERIAN ISLANDS

OSTROV
KOTEL'NYY

OSTROV NOVAYA
SIBIR'

OSTROV BOL'SHOY
LYAKHOVSKIY

OSTROV TAYMYR
GORY BYRRANGA

LAPTEV
SEA

E A S T   S I B E R I A N
S E A

CHUKCHI
SEA

Bering Strait

OSTROV
VRANGELYA

CHUKOTSKIY
POLUOSTROV

BERING
SEA

Providentya
Anadyr'

mys Navarin

mys Shelagskiy

Arctic Circle

Markovo

ANYUYSKIY KHREBET

mys Svyatoy Nos

mys Buor-
Khaya

Ambarchik

Omolon

gora Pobeda
10,325 Ft.

Kolyma

gora Izvestkovaya
8,406 Ft.

Klyuchi

Kovacha

Tiksi

Kazach'ye

Srednekolymsk

Indirka

Yana

NTRAL

gora Kamen'
581 Ft.

ERIAN

Yessey

IBERIA

Nizhnyaya Tunguska

Khatanga

Zhigansk

Lena

VERKHOYANSKIY   KHREBET

Pik Aborigen
8,184 Ft.

Magadan

mys Tolstoy

OSTROV KARAGINSKIY

OSTROV KOMANDORSKIYE OSTROVA

Klyuchevskaya Sopka
15,584 Ft.

OSTROV
BERINGA

OSTROV
MEDNYJ

SREDINNYY   KHREBET

Petropavlovsk-Kamchatskiy

mys Shipunskiy

I A

Yakutsk

Lena

Monkoka

Vil'uj

Aldan

SEA
OF
OKHOTSK

vulkan Ichinskaya Sopka
11,880 Ft.

POLUOSTROV
KAMCHATKA

mys Lopatka

OSTROV PARAMUSHIR

Lensk

ALDANSKOYE
NAGOR'YE

KHREBET DZHUGDZHUR

Ayan

Okhotsk

mys Yelizavety

mys Yuzhno-Kamchatskiy

OSTROV ONEKOTAN

Angara

Ust'-Ilimsk

gora Inyaptuk
8,458 Ft.

STANOVOY KHREBET

Neryungri

Tynda

Nikolayevsk-na-Amure

Amur

Okha

SAKHALIN

gora Lopatina
5,279 Ft.

Tatar Strait

mys Terpeniya

KURIL ISLANDS

OSTROV SIMUSHIR

OSTROV URUP

Ust'-Kut

Bratsk

Vizhneudinsk

STANOVOYE
NAGOR'YE

Vitum

Svobodnyy

Komsomol'sk-
na-Amure

Sovetskaya
Gavan'

OSTROV ITURUP

Zima

Lena

Lake
Baikal

Vitim

Blagoveshchensk

Birobidzhan

gora Tardoki-Jani
6,814 Ft.

Yuzhno-Sakhalinsk

Korsakov

OSTROV KUNASHIR

Usolye-Sibirskoye

Chita

Khabarovsk

La Perouse Strait

Angarsk
Irkutsk   Ulan-Ude

gora Munku-Sardyk
11,453 Ft.

Selenge

Borzya

SIKHOTE-ALIN

Orhon

Ulan Bator

Choybalsan

Ussuriysk

Vladivostok

Nakhodka

O N G O L I A

Erdene

O B I

0   100   200   300   400   500 Miles
0   200   400   600   800 Kilometers

Scale 1:24,000,000; one inch to 379 miles

Copyright by Rand McNally & Co.
Made in U.S.A.
N-CMW60091-P1- -1-1-1

Many people in Central Asia live in
yurts—circular tents covered with
animal hides.

The train station at
Vladivostok, Russia,
marks the eastern end
of the Trans-Siberian
Railroad. The route
begins in Moscow
and runs 5,800 miles
(9,280 kilometers)
through Russia.

Cotton, one of Central Asia's
main cash crops, is grown on flat
grasslands known as "steppes."

A man in Uzbekistan engraves
ornate patterns into decorative
plates.

Siberian tigers can
withstand the brutal cold
of northern winters.

EAST ASIA

Tokyo, Japan, is the most populous city in the world.

China, the most populous country in the world and the third-largest in land area, dominates East Asia. Much of western China's landscape is harsh and barren, encompassing the high, rugged Tibetan Plateau and two vast deserts, the Gobi and the Takla Makan. Most of China's people live in the eastern part of the country, where there are fertile plains, river valleys, and deltas. Japan is a mountainous island country. Although little of its land is suitable for farming, rice grows in lowland areas and on terraced hillsides. Despite having few natural resources, Japan has become one of the world's wealthiest and most highly industrialized countries.

South Korea and North Korea occupy a peninsula east of China. Once a single, united country, Korea was divided into North and South Korea following World War II. South Korea has most of the farmland, while North Korea is highly industrialized.

With an excellent natural harbor, Kaosiung is the fastest-growing city in Taiwan.

Kabuki Theater in Japan dates back to the early 1600s.

ALTAI

JUNGGAR PENDI

Yining

Manas

ÜRÜMQI

TIEN SHAN

Pik Pobedy
24,406 Ft.

Kashi

Aksu

Hami

BEI SHAN

Shache

TARIM PENDI

Hotan

QILIAN SHAN

Yumen

Zhangye

K2
28,250 Ft.

ALTUN SHAN

Wuwei

KUNLUN SHAN

△ Muztag
25,338 Ft.

QAIDAM PENDI

Golmud

Qinghai Hu

Xining

LANZHOU

Bangong Co

△ Leli Shan
21,020 Ft.

PLATEAU

△ Yagradagzê Shan
17,854 Ft.

A'NYÊMAQEN SHAN

Kangrinboqê Feng
△ 22,028 Ft.

OF TIBET

BAYAN HAR SHAN

Huang

CHINA

Tia

HIMALAYAS

GANGDISÊ SHAN

Nam Co

Salween

Guang

Guanxian   Nanc

CHENGDU

Suin

Xigazê   Lhasa

Brahmaputra

Namjagbarwa Feng
25,446 Ft.

Gongga Shan
24,790 Ft.△

Yangtze

Zi

Mt. Everest
△ 29,028 Ft.

Wutongqiao

Y

Xichang

Zhaoton

KUNMING

Mekong

Ans

Baoshan

Tonghai

Wensha

Gejiu

Tropic of Cancer

10   11   12   13   14   15   16   17

N W E S

SEA OF OKHOTSK

La Perouse Strait

GREATER KHINGAN RANGE

MANCHURIA

Manzhouli
Hailar
Hulun Nur
Ergun
Gen
Nonni
Amur
Bei'an
Yichun
Hegang
QIQIHAR
Suihua
Jiamusi
Shuangyashan
Songhua
Jixi
Horqin Youyi Qianqi
Baicheng
Nen
HARBIN
Mudanjiang
CHANGCHUN
JILIN
Tongliao
Liaoyuan
Wangqing
Siping
Erenhot
Chifeng
Fuxin
FUSHUN
Tonghua
Liao
Ch'öngjin
SEA OF JAPAN
Hyesan
Hohhot
Jining
Chengde
Jinzhou
Yingkou
SHENYANG
Benxi
Sinŭiju
Yalu
Kimch'aek
BAOTOU
Zhangjiakou
BEIJING
Qinhuangdao
Dandong
Hŭngnam
NORTH KOREA
Datong
TANGSHAN
P'YŎNGYANG
Wŏnsan
Korea Bay
Namp'o
Yulin
TIANJIN
DALIAN
Kaesŏng
SEOUL
Baoding
Cangzhou
Bo Hai
Haeju
INCH'ŎN
TAIYUAN
SHIJIAZHUANG
Yantai
TAEJŎN
TAEGU
Yangquan
Weifang
Chŏnju
Ulsan
SOUTH KOREA
Handan
QINGDAO
PUSAN
Yonago
Changzhi
JINAN
Boshan
KWANGJU
HIROSHIMA
Jiaozuo
Xinxiang
Jining
Linyi
Mokp'o
KITAKYŪSHŪ
Luoyang
Kaifeng
Lianyungang
YELLOW SEA
Cheju
FUKUOKA
Pingdingshan
ZHENGZHOU
Shangqiu
Xuzhou
CHEJU-DO (S. Korea)
Nagasaki
Kumamoto
Luohe
Nanyang
Bengbu
Huainan
Zhenjiang
Nantong
KYŪSHŪ
Miyazaki
Xinyang
NANJING
SHANGHAI
Kagoshima
Hefei
Wuhu
Wuxi
YAKU-SHIMA
TANEGA-SHIMA
WUHAN
Anqing
HANGZHOU
Huangshi
Shaoxing
Ningbo
EAST CHINA SEA
CHANGDE
Nanchang
Jiujiang
Jingdezhen
Shangrao
Linhai
Wenzhou
Yiyang
CHANGSHA
Poyang Hu
Fuzhou
WUYI SHAN
Xiangtan
Pingxiang
Nanping
Shaoyang
Hengyang
Chenxian
Ganzhou
Fuzhou
T'AIPEI
Guilin
Shaoguan
Quanzhou
Hsinchu
Liuzhou
Zhangzhou
Hsinchu
T'aichung
Wuzhou
Xiamen
Chiai
Chao'an
Xun
Foshan
Shantou
T'ainan
Nanning
Yulin
Jiangmen
GUANGZHOU
KAOHSIUNG
TAIWAN
Maoming
Macau
HONG KONG (XIANGGANG)
Oluan Pi
Zhanjiang
LEIZHOU BANDAO
TUNGSHA TAO (Claimed by China, Taiwan)
Luzon Strait
Gulf of Tonkin
Haikou
HAINAN DAO
Wuzhi Shan 6,125 Ft.
SOUTH CHINA SEA

HOKKAIDŌ
Nayoro
Asahikawa
Kushiro
SAPPORO
Obihiro
Murorah
Erimo-misaki
Hakodate
Hachinohe
Aomori
Morioka
HONSHŪ
Akita
Sakata
Sendai
Niigata
Fukushima
Iwaki
JAPAN
Toyama
Nagano
Utsunomiya
Kanazawa
Maebashi
TŌKYŌ
Fukui
NAGOYA
YOKOHAMA
KYŌTO
Mt. Fuji 12,388 Ft.
KOBE
OSAKA
Hamamatsu
Wakayama
IZU ISLANDS
Ōita
Kōchi
SHIKOKU
PACIFIC OCEAN
AMAM-O-SHIMA
TOKUNO-SHIMA
RYUKYU ISLANDS
OKINAWA-JIMA
Naha
Tropic of Cancer
IRIOMOTE-JIMA
MIYAKO-JIMA
ISHIGAKI-SHIMA

Korea Strait
OKI-SHOTO

Yu Shan 13,114 Ft.

100 200 300 400 500 Miles
200 400 600 800 Kilometers
Scale 1:20,000,000; one inch to 315 miles
Copyright by Rand McNally & Co.
Made in U.S.A.
N-CMW66100-P1- -1-1-1

Mount Fuji's snowcapped summit rises above a tea plantation in central Japan.

Giant pandas still live in the bamboo forests of central China.

Almost all of the world's large-scale silk production takes place in Asia, where shops like this one in South Korea display hundreds of brightly-colored fabric bolts.

Bicycles are a popular way to travel through the crowded streets of Chinese cities.

SOUTHEAST ASIA

Hot, humid Southeast Asia consists of an enormous peninsula–known as Indochina–and some 20,000 islands. Rice is the major crop, but other tropical crops grow here, too. Palm oil from Malaysia, rubber from Indonesia, coconuts and sugarcane from the Philippines, and hardwoods from throughout the region contribute significantly to the regional economy. Mineral resources, including oil, coal, natural gas, and tin, are also abundant. In fact, oil and natural gas reserves in Brunei have made this small country one of the world's richest. In recent years, tiny Singapore has become an important international center of business and finance.

Thailand's long coast is lined with many secluded inlets, like this one near Phuket.

Bicycles are the best way for fruit vendors in Hanoi, Vietnam, to distribute their produce.

INDIAN OCEAN

10   11   12   13   14   15   16   17

A family of monkeys sits in front of a temple in Myanmar.

A low sun illuminates the silhouettes of Buddhist temples in Myanmar.

Two cattle pull a farmer through a rice paddy in Bali, Indonesia.

Elementary schoolchildren play in Zamboanga, on the Philippine island of Mindanao.

Kuala Lumpur began as a small mining settlement, but today it is the bustling capital of Malaysia.

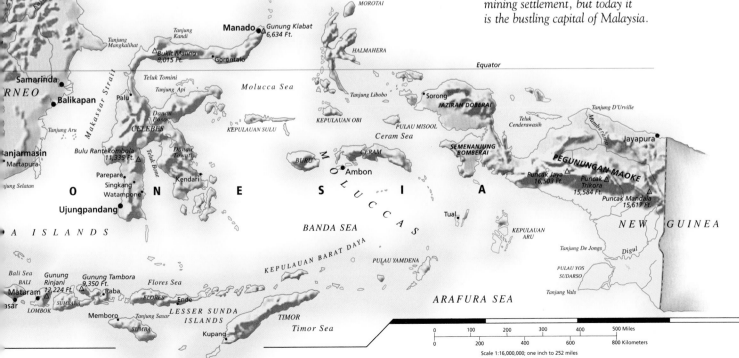

N W E S

Luzon Strait

BABUYAN ISLANDS

Mayraira Point

Laoag

Escarpada Point

Vigan

Ilagan

San Fernando

LUZON

Baguio

SIERRA MADRE

Dagupan

Tarlac

Cabanatuan

Angeles

P H I L I P P I N E

S E A

MANILA ⊛ Quezon City

Laguna de Bay

Lucena   Naga

Legaspi

MINDORO

Bohol Sea

SAMAR

PHILIPPINES

Libro Point

PANAY

LEYTE

Tacloban

Iloilo

Bacolod

Cebu

NEGROS

Tagbilaran

PALAWAN

Puerto
Princesa

Dumaguete

Sibuyan Sea

Butuan

Cagayan de Oro

Pagadian

Marawi

Bislig

MINDANAO

Davao

Cotabato

Mount Apo
9,692 Ft.

Cape San Agustin

Zamboanga

Koronadal

General Santos

Jolo

Tinaca Point

S O U T H

C H I N A   S E A

SULU SEA

Balabac Strait

*Gunong Kinabalu
13,455 Ft.*

Kinabalu

Sandakan

Tanjong Hog

Tawau

Bandar Seri Begawan

Tarakan

CELEBES SEA

KEPULAUAN TALAUD

MOROTAI

Manado   Gunung Klabat
6,634 Ft.

Tanjung Kandi

Tanjung Mangkalihat

*Bukit Malino
8,015 Ft.*

Gorontalo

HALMAHERA

Equator

Samarinda

Teluk Tomini

Molucca Sea

Balikpapan

Tanjung Api

Tanjung Libobo

Sorong

JAZIRAH DOBERAI

Tanjung D'Urville

Danau Poso

CELEBES

KEPULAUAN OBI

PULAU MISOOL

Teluk Cenderawasih

Mamberamo

Jayapura

Tanjung Aru

BORNEO

Palu

KEPULAUAN SULU

Ceram Sea

SEMENANJUNG BOMBERAI

Banjarmasin

*Bulu Rantekombola
11,335 Ft.*

Teluk Bone

Danau Towuti

CERAM

PEGUNUNGAN MAOKE

Martapura

BURU

Ambon

Puncak Jaya
16,503 Ft.

Puncak Trikora
15,584 Ft.

Parepare

Singkang

Kendari

M O L U C C A S

Puncak Mandala
15,617 Ft.

Tanjung Selatan

Watampone

I N D O N E S I A

NEW   GUINEA

Ujungpandang

Tual

KEPULAUAN ARU

Tanjung De Jongs

A   I S L A N D S

BANDA SEA

Digul

KEPULAUAN BARAT DAYA

PULAU YAMDENA

*PULAU YOS
SUDARSO*

Tanjung Vals

Bali Sea

BALI

Gunung Rinjani
12,224 Ft.

Gunung Tambora
9,350 Ft.

Flores Sea

Mataram

Raba

ARAFURA SEA

LOMBOK

SUMBAWA

FLORES

Ende

LESSER SUNDA ISLANDS

TIMOR

Timor Sea

Memboro

Tanjung Sasar

SUMBA

Kupang

PACIFIC OCEAN

| 0 | 100 | 200 | 300 | 400 | 500 Miles |
| 0 | 200 | 400 | 600 | 800 Kilometers |

Scale 1:16,000,000; one inch to 252 miles
Copyright by Rand McNally & Co.
Made in U.S.A.

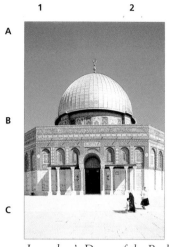

Jerusalem's Dome of the Rock is an important Muslim shrine.

Saudi Arabia's Ar Rub' al Khāli, or "The Empty Quarter," contains mountainous sand ridges.

Caspian Sea

Khvoy · Ahar · Marand
Orūmīyeh · Tabrīz · Ardabīl
Al-Qāmishlī
Lake Urmia · Mīāneh
HALAB · Ar Raqqah · Al Mawsil · Irbil · Marāgheh · Rasht
Al Lādhiqīyah · Idlib · Hamāh · Zanjān · Gonbad-e Qābūs · Qūchān
Tartūs · Ţarābulus · Hamāh · Dayr az Zawr · As Sulaymānayah · Mahābād · Qazvīn · Karaj · Āmol · Sārī · ELBURZ MTS. · Sabzevār · MASH
Ţarţūs · Himṣ · Karkūk · Sanandaj · Qolleh-ye Damāvand 18,386 Ft. · Neyshābūr
LEBANON · Sayda · Beirut · SYRIA · Euphrates · Bākhtarān · Hamādān · Qom · Torbat-e Heydarīyeh
ISRAEL · Haifa · DAMASCUS · BAGHDĀD · Borūjerd · Arāk · TEHRĀN · DASHT-E KAVĪR
Tel Aviv-Yafo · Teverya · Irbid · IRAQ · Ar Ramādī · Khorramābād · Kāshān · Ardakān · Birjand
Gaza · Az-Zarqā' · Amman · Al Hillah · Dezful · Najafābād · Eṣfahān · Yazd · Zābo
Be'ér Sheva · Jerusalem · An Najaf · Al 'Amārah · Masjed-e Soleymān · Qomsheh · Daryācheh-ye Hāmūn
JORDAN · Dead Sea · An Nāṣirīyah · Ahvāz · IRAN · Kermān · Zāhedān
Jabal Ramm △ 5,755 Ft. · Hawr al-Hammar · Basra · ZAGROS MTS. · Shīrāz · Bam
Jabal Al Lawz △ 7,884 Ft. · Abādān · KUWAIT · BŪBIYĀN · Jahrom
Gulf of Aqaba · Tabūk · Al Jahrah · Kuwait · Bandar-e Bushehr · Bandar-e 'Abbās
Ra's Abu Madd · AN NAFŪD · Hā'il · Persian Gulf · JAZIREH-YE QESHM · Strait of Hormuz
AL-HIJAZ · Buraydah · Ad Dammām · BAHRAIN · Ra's al-Khaymah · OMAN
SAUDI ARABIA · Al Khubar · Al Manāmah · QATAR · Ash Shāriqah · Gulf of Oman
Medina · AD DAHNĀ · Al Hufūf · Ad Dawḥah · Dubayy · Al 'Ayn
RIYADH · UNITED ARAB EMIRATES · Abu Dhabi · Muscat
JIDDAH · Mecca · ARABIAN PENINSULA · Jabal ash-Shām △ 9,957 Ft. · Sūr · Ra's al Hadd
At Tā'if · OMAN · MAṢĪRAH
RED SEA · Jabal Sawdā' △ 10,522 Ft. · AR RUB' AL KHĀLI · Khalīj Maṣīrah
'Asīr · Abhā · Khamis Mushayt · Ra's al Madrakha
Abā as Su'ūd · Dawḥat Ṣawqirah
Ṣa'dah · Ṣalālah
an-Nabī Shu'ayb · Ghubbat al Qamar · Ra's Fartak
Jabal 12,008 Ft. · Sanaa · YEMEN
Al Hudaydah · Ta'izz · Al Mukallā
Bab el Mandeb · Aden · SOCOTRA (Yemen)
Gulf of Aden

MEDITERRANEAN SEA

INDIA

SOUTH ASIA AND THE MIDDLE EAST

South Asia is separated from the rest of Asia by the highest mountains in the world: the Himalayas, the Karakoram Range and the Hindu Kush. Nepal and Bhutan lie tilted along the southern slopes of the Himalayas, their land rising steeply from low plains and foothills up to the loftiest mountaintops. To the south is India, the second-most populous country in the world, after China. To the west of South Asia is the Middle East. Deserts cover much of this region, but beneath the desert sands lies a fortune in oil and natural gas. These resources have made many Middle Eastern countries wealthy, but have also sparked conflict in the region.

Soldiers enjoy a meal in Afghanistan.

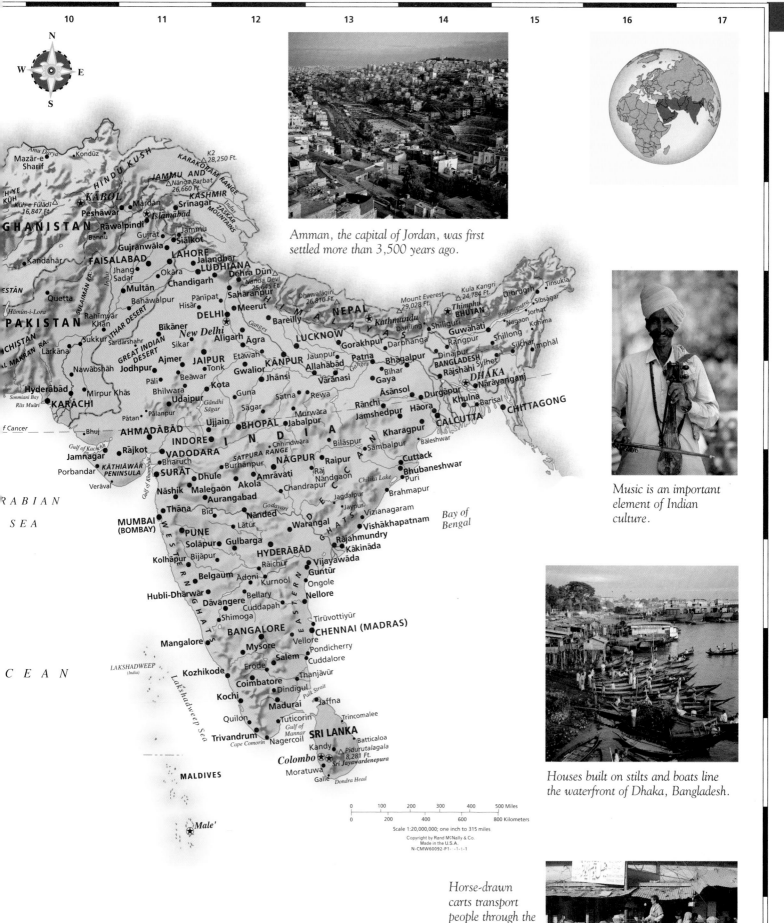

Amman, the capital of Jordan, was first settled more than 3,500 years ago.

Music is an important element of Indian culture.

Houses built on stilts and boats line the waterfront of Dhaka, Bangladesh.

Horse-drawn carts transport people through the crowded streets of Lahore, Pakistan.

Scale 1:20,000,000; one inch to 315 miles
Copyright by Rand McNally & Co.
Made in the U.S.A.
N-CMW60092-P1- -1-1-1

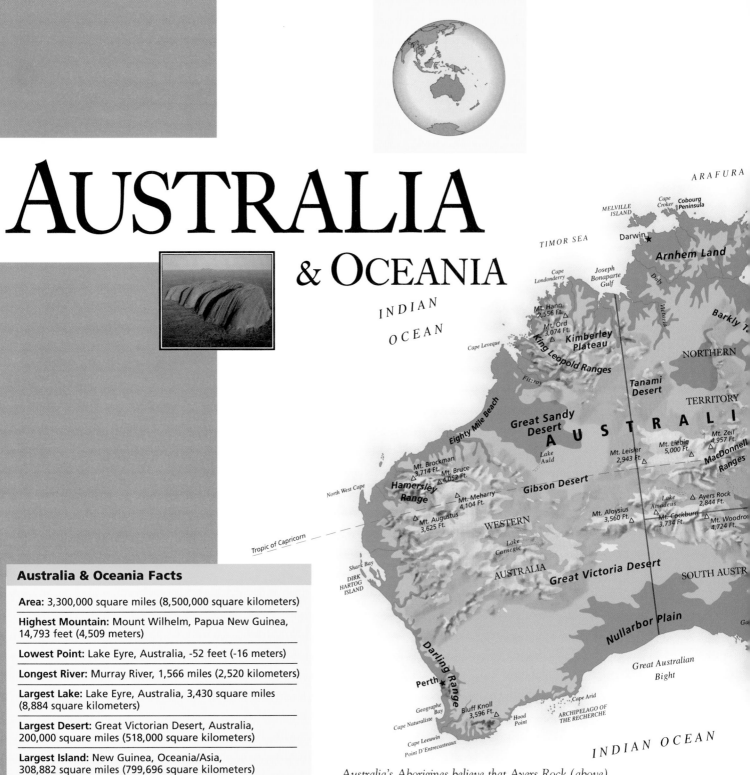

AUSTRALIA
& OCEANIA

INDIAN

OCEAN

ARAFURA

MELVILLE
ISLAND

Cape
Croker
Cobourg
Peninsula

TIMOR SEA

Darwin ★

Arnhem Land

Cape
Londonderry

Joseph
Bonaparte
Gulf

Daly

Victoria

Barkly T

Mt. Hann
2,556 Ft.

Mt. Ord
3,074 Ft.

Kimberley
Plateau

NORTHERN

Cape Leveque

King Leopold Ranges

Tanami
Desert

TERRITORY

Fitzroy

Great Sandy
Desert

A U S T R A L I

Mt. Zeil
4,957 Ft.

Eighty Mile Beach

Lake
Auld

Mt. Leister
2,943 Ft.

Mt. Liebig
5,000 Ft.

MacDonnell
Ranges

North West Cape

Mt. Brockman
3,714 Ft.

Mt. Bruce
4,052 Ft.

Hamersley
Range

Gibson Desert

Lake
Amadeus

Ayers Rock
2,844 Ft.

Mt. Meharry
4,104 Ft.

Mt. Aloysius
3,560 Ft.

Mt. Cockburn
3,734 Ft.

Mt. Woodro
4,724 Ft.

Mt. Augustus
3,625 Ft.

WESTERN

Tropic of Capricorn

Lake
Carnegie

Shark Bay

AUSTRALIA

Great Victoria Desert

SOUTH AUSTR

DIRK
HARTOG
ISLAND

Nullarbor Plain

Australia & Oceania Facts

Area: 3,300,000 square miles (8,500,000 square kilometers)

Highest Mountain: Mount Wilhelm, Papua New Guinea, 14,793 feet (4,509 meters)

Lowest Point: Lake Eyre, Australia, -52 feet (-16 meters)

Longest River: Murray River, 1,566 miles (2,520 kilometers)

Largest Lake: Lake Eyre, Australia, 3,430 square miles (8,884 square kilometers)

Largest Desert: Great Victorian Desert, Australia, 200,000 square miles (518,000 square kilometers)

Largest Island: New Guinea, Oceania/Asia, 308,882 square miles (799,696 square kilometers)

Darling Range

Perth ★

Great Australian
Bight

Cape Arid

Geographe
Bay

Bluff Knoll
3,596 Ft.

Hood
Point

ARCHIPELAGO OF
THE RECHERCHE

Cape Naturaliste

Cape Leeuwin
Point D'Entrecasteaux

INDIAN OCEAN

Australia's Aborigines believe that Ayers Rock (above) is sacred; Sydney, Australia (below), is built around one of the world's largest natural harbors.

"**A**ustralia" has two meanings. It is the name of both the world's smallest, flattest continent and the world's sixth-largest country, which occupies the entire continent. It is the only inhabited continent that lies completely within the southern hemisphere; for this reason it has been nicknamed "The Land Down Under." Most of Australia's interior–the Outback–is barren desert, sparsely populated but ruggedly beautiful, with dramatic landforms such as Ayers Rock. Australia's best-known geographic feature, however, is the Great Barrier Reef, Earth's largest living structure, which stretches 1,250 miles (2,000 kilometers) through the Coral Sea off Australia's eastern coast.

To the north and east of Australia lies Oceania, which is made up of more than 25,000 volcanic islands and coral atolls scattered across the Pacific Ocean. A few of the islands, such as New Guinea and New Zealand's North and South Islands, are relatively large, but many others are too small to appear on any but the most detailed maps.

Land Elevation
Feet (Meters)

9,840 and over (3,000 and over)
6,560 - 9,840 (2,000 - 3,000)
3,280 - 6,560 (1,000 - 2,000)
1,640 - 3,280 (500 - 1,000)
656 - 1,640 (200 - 500)
0 - 656 feet (0 - 200)

Scale 1:20,000,000; one inch to 315 miles

Copyright by Rand McNally & Co.
Made in U.S.A.
N-CMW95000-A1- -1-1-1

Torres Strait
Cape York
Cape York Peninsula
CORAL SEA
Gulf of Carpentaria
Bartle Frere 5,322 Ft.
Gregory Range
Great Barrier Reef
Halifax Bay
Clarke Range
Great Dividing Range
△ Mt. Dalrymple 4,131 Ft.
Selwyn Range
Great Artesian Basin
QUEENSLAND
Simpson Desert
Cape Capricorn
Tropic of Capricorn
Sandy Cape
FRASER ISLAND
PACIFIC OCEAN
Cooper Creek
Grey Range
Mt. Kiangarow △ 3,760 Ft.
Darling Downs
★ Brisbane
Southport
Cape Byron
Sturt Stony Desert
Lake Eyre North
Barwon
Lake Torrens
Barrier Range
Darling
NEW SOUTH WALES
Penrith
Newcastle
Sydney
Mary Peak 3,871 Ft.
Murray
Lachlan
Wollongong
Canberra A.C.T. ⊛
Jervis Bay
★ Adelaide
Vincent
Encounter KANGAROO Bay ISLAND
VICTORIA
Snowy Mts △ Mt. Kosciuszko 7,313 Ft.
Cape Jaffa
Cape Howe
Cape Nelson
★ Melbourne
Cape Otway
Wilsons Promontory
Bass Strait
KING ISLAND
FLINDERS ISLAND
Cape Grim
Cape Portland
TASMAN SEA
Mt. Ossa 5,305 Ft.
Freycinet Peninsula
TASMANIA
★ Hobart
South East Cape

NORFOLK ISLAND

North Cape
Auckland
Needles Point
NORTH ISLAND
Bay of Plenty
Cape Egmont
East Cape
△ Mt. Ruapehu 9,177 Ft.
Cape Farewell
The Twins 5,990 Ft.
NEW ZEALAND
Cook Strait
⊛ Wellington
Aoraki 12,316 Ft.
Southern Alps
Christchurch
SOUTH ISLAND
Banks Peninsula
Cape Providence
Dunedin
Foveaux Strait
CHATHAM ISLANDS
STEWART ISLAND

N
W   E
S

0 100 200 300 400 500 Miles
0 200 400 600 800 Kilometers

THE LAND

Desert wastelands of sand and rock blanket the central and western parts of Australia, while a broad band of dry grasslands surrounds the deserts. Only about six percent of Australia's land is suitable for farming. Most Australians live along the southeastern coast, between the ocean and the long chain of mountains and plateaus known as the Great Dividing Range. Manufacturing and service industries flourish in this region. New Zealand, Australia's neighbor to the southeast, includes mountains, fjords, glaciers, rain forests, and geysers. Thanks to its small population and lack of heavy industry, it is one of the least polluted countries in the world. New Guinea, which lies to the north of Australia, is the second-largest island in the world. High, jagged mountains form a long spine across its width, wide swampy plains line its coasts, and tropical rain forests cover much of the island. Most of the other islands of Oceania were formed by volcanoes.

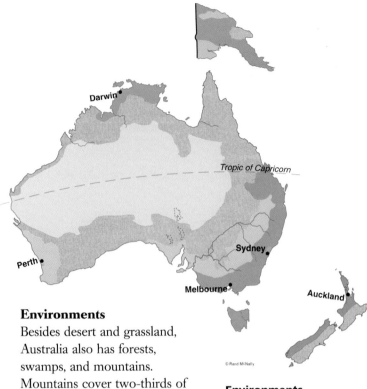

Environments

Besides desert and grassland, Australia also has forests, swamps, and mountains. Mountains cover two-thirds of New Zealand. New Guinea's dense rain forests, with their valuable hardwood trees, are an important natural resource, as are the palm trees that grow on many of the other islands of Oceania.

Environments

- Forest
- Swamp
- Crop and woodland
- Cropland
- Crop and grazing land
- Grassland
- Desert
- Tundra
- Barren
- Urban

Mineral processing facilities can be found throughout Australia.

Manufacturing

Manufacturing plays a central role in Australia's economy, with the refinement of metals and other natural resources topping the list of industries. The country also produces chemicals, plastics, textiles, and other durable goods. Traditionally, New Zealand has produced few manufactured goods, but its food-processing and paper manufacturing industries have been expanding. Most of the other countries in Oceania do not produce manufactured goods.

Sheep outnumber people in Australia by a ratio of seven to one. In New Zealand, the ratio is 14 to 1.

Much of Australia's interior, called the Outback, consists of semiarid plains that harbor hearty plants and animals.

Wool

With more than 14 percent of the world's sheep, Australia produces more wool than any other country on Earth. The largest sheep "stations," or ranches, cover more than 5,000 square miles (12,900 square kilometers). New Zealand ranks as the second-largest wool producer; nearly half of its land is used as pasture.

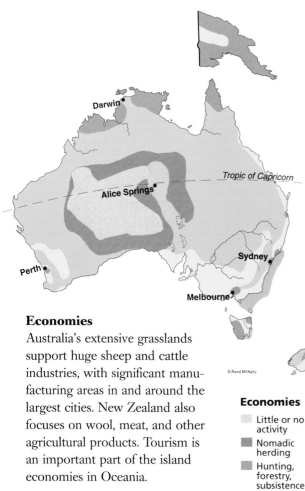

Economies

Australia's extensive grasslands support huge sheep and cattle industries, with significant manufacturing areas in and around the largest cities. New Zealand also focuses on wool, meat, and other agricultural products. Tourism is an important part of the island economies in Oceania.

Economies

Miners sift through mounds of sediment to uncover opals, iridescent gemstones that are exported.

- Little or no activity
- Nomadic herding
- Hunting, forestry, subsistence farming
- Forestry
- Agriculture
- Stock raising
- Manufacturing, commerce
- Fishing

Gems and Minerals

White, black, and fire opals mined in southern Australia are world-famous, but Australia is also an important source of diamonds: Its mines produce thirty percent of the world's supply. Australia's many other mineral resources include iron ore, coal, uranium, lead, zinc, copper, nickel, and natural gas. New Zealand has large reserves of coal, natural gas, and oil, while New Guinea's greatest sources of mineral wealth are copper, gold, and silver.

Not all diamonds become jewelry; industries use them to cut hard surfaces.

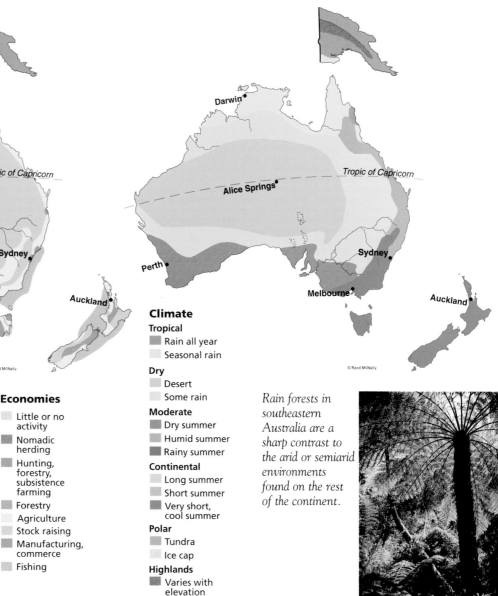

Climate

Tropical
- Rain all year
- Seasonal rain

Dry
- Desert
- Some rain

Moderate
- Dry summer
- Humid summer
- Rainy summer

Continental
- Long summer
- Short summer
- Very short, cool summer

Polar
- Tundra
- Ice cap

Highlands
- Varies with elevation

Rain forests in southeastern Australia are a sharp contrast to the arid or semiarid environments found on the rest of the continent.

Climate

In central and western Australia, the climate is very hot and dry. Near the coasts, especially in the southeast and the north, rain is more abundant and temperatures are cooler. New Zealand's climate is generally milder and wetter than Australia's. New Guinea and most other parts of Oceania have hot tropical climates.

Tourism

Tourists are drawn to Australia's natural wonders as well as to the fun-loving, easygoing lifestyle of Australians. Scenic New Zealand also enjoys a booming tourist industry. The tropical islands of Oceania have long been popular vacation spots, especially for sun-seeking Europeans and Americans.

Airplanes provide a spectacular view of the Great Barrier Reef.

THE PEOPLE

Although Australia is one of the largest countries in the world, it has a relatively small population. Very few people live in its vast interior–the Outback. Most Australians live near the coast, especially along the southeastern stretch that includes Sydney, Melbourne, Brisbane, and Adelaide. Although the Aborigines were the earliest humans to settle the continent, they make up only one percent of Australia's population today. Most Australians are descendants of British settlers, but in recent years immigrants from all over the world have added diversity to the continent's ethnic makeup. New Zealand's population is similar to Australia's, but its native people, the Maoris, represent ten percent of the population. Due to centuries of isolation, the island groups of Oceania have retained their distinct cultures. There has been little immigration there from other parts of the world.

The Aborigine culture includes many ceremonial dances and rituals.

A father and son ride around their farm in Australia.

Boating is a popular pastime for tourists in Australia and New Zealand.

Australia's large population of kangaroos often comes into contact with humans.

Map labels

ARAFURA SEA

MELVILLE ISLAND Cape Croker

Van Diemen Gulf

Darwin

Arnhem Land

Pine Creek

TIMOR SEA

Cape Londonderry

Joseph Bonaparte Gulf

Mataranka

Wyndham

Kimberley Plateau

NORTHERN

INDIAN OCEAN

Cape Leveque

Yeeda

Halls Creek

Hooker Creek

Broome

Fitzroy

Christmas Creek

The Granites

Tennant Cre

Cape Latouche Treville

TERRITORY

Port Hedland

Marble Bar

Great Sandy Desert

AUSTRALI

Dampier

Nullagine

Lake Auld

Alice Sprin

Yarraloola

Ethel Creek

Lake Amadeus

Onslow

Ayers Rock 2,844 Ft.

North West Cape

WESTERN

Minilya

Carnegie

Tropic of Capricorn

Carnarvon

Lake Carnegie

SOUTH AUSTRALL

Wooramel

Wiluna

AUSTRALIA

Shark Bay

Meekatharra

Mount E

DIRK HARTOG ISLAND

Sandstone

White Cliffs

Kingoonya

Mount Magnet

Leonora

Great Victoria Desert

Mullewa

Paynes Find

Geraldton

Dongara

Kalgoorlie-Boulder

Eucla

Ceduna

Gaire

Streaky Bay

Coolgardie

Norseman

Balladonia

Great Australian Bight

Wanneroo

Gosnells

Port L

Perth

Armadale

Cape C

Fremantle

Newdegate

Wagin

Hopetoun

Cape Arid

Geographe Bay

Bunbury

Hood Point

ARCHIPELAGO OF THE RECHERCHE

Cape Naturaliste

Augusta

Point D'Entrecasteaux

Cranbrook

Albany

Darling Range

INDIAN OCEAN

Victoria

Dali

Newcastle Waters

GR EY

10   11   12   13   14   15   16   17

The Aborigines developed boomerangs to aid them in hunting animals.

Australia & Oceania Facts

Population: 29,900,000

Population Density: 9.1 people per square mile (3.5 per square kilometer)

Most Populous Country: Australia, 18,735,000 people

Largest City: Sydney, Australia, 3,740,000 people (metropolitan area)

These schoolgirls in Sydney exhibit Australia's easygoing manner.

Torres Strait
Cape York
Bamaga
Duifken Point
Weipa
Cape York Peninsula
Gulf of Carpentaria
own
Cooktown
CORAL SEA
Normanton
Cairns
Halifax Bay
Townsville
hoooweal
nt Isa
Cloncurry
Hughenden
Mackay
Winton
Blair Athol
Cape Capricorn
Great Artesian Basin
Longreach
Barcaldine
Emerald
Rockhampton
Springsure
Gladstone
Yaraka
Blackall
Theodore
Bundaberg
Tropic of Capricorn
QUEENSLAND
Maryborough
Sandy Cape
Charleville
Mitchell
FRASER ISLAND
Innamincka
Thargomindah
Chinchilla
Toowoomba
Gympie
PACIFIC
Cunnamulla
Redcliffe
Ipswich
★**Brisbane**
OCEAN
Warwick
Southport
ike Eyre orth
Milparinka
Bourke
Lismore
Cape Byron
Marree
Armidale
Grafton
Darling
Tamworth
Coffs Harbour
ke rrens
Broken Hill
Nyngan
Taree
NORFOLK ISLAND
(Austl.)
ort Augusta
Wilcannia
Dubbo
Newcastle
walla
NEW SOUTH WALES
Cessnock
Port Pirie
Penrith
●**Sydney**
Mildura
Griffith
Campbelltown
Elizabeth
Goulburn
Wollongong
Wagga Wagga
A.C.T.
●**Adelaide**
Canberra
Jervis Bay
VICTORIA
Albury
Encounter
Wangaratta
00 Bay
Bendigo
Cooma
Cape Jaffa
Horsham
Mt. Kosciuszko 7,313 Ft.
Ballarat
Cape Howe
Hamilton
Geelong
★**Melbourne**
Mount Gambier
Portland
Moe
Sale
Cape Otway
Wilsons Promontory
TASMAN
KING ISLAND
Bass Strait
FLINDERS ISLAND
SEA
Cape Grim
Burnie
Devonport
Zeehan
Launceston
TASMANIA
★Hobart
South East Cape

NORTH ISLAND
North Cape
Whangarei
East Coast Bays
Manukau
●**Auckland**
Hamilton
Bay of Plenty
Tauranga
New Plymouth
Cape Egmont
Taupo
Rotorua
East Cape
Wanganui
Gisborne
Napier
Cape Farewell
Hastings
Palmerston North
Nelson
Porirua
Greymouth
●**Wellington**
Aoraki 12,316 Ft.
Cook Strait
SOUTH ISLAND
Haast
Waiau
NEW ZEALAND
Southern Alps
●**Christchurch**
Cape Providence
Ashburton
Manapouri
Oamaru
CHATHAM ISLANDS (N.Z.)
Invercargill
Foveaux Strait
Dunedin
STEWART ISLAND

0   100   200   300   400   500 Miles
0   200   400   600   800 Kilometers

Scale 1:20,000,000; one inch to 315 miles
Copyright by Rand McNally & Co.
Made in U.S.A.
N-CMW95000-P1- -:-1-1-1

PACIFIC ISLANDS

Scattered across a vast area in the Pacific Ocean, the islands of Oceania feature landscapes as varied as the alpine terrain of New Zealand's South Island, the mountain rain forests of Papua New Guinea, and the flower- and palm-strewn atolls of Polynesia. Papua New Guinea, which occupies the western portion of the island of New Guinea, is Oceania's largest country. It is a land of broad ethnic variety: More than 700 dialects are spoken there, although English is the official language. To the east of Papua New Guinea lies the group of islands known as Melanesia, a name that means "black islands." To the north and east of Melanesia is Micronesia, which means "small islands," and farther east lies Polynesia, or "many islands." These far-flung volcanic islands and coral atolls were originally settled by seafaring peoples from the Asian mainland who brought their plants, animals, and cultures with them as they ventured as far as Hawaii and Easter Island in huge canoes.

B
C
D
E
F
G
H
I
J
K

PHILIPPINE SEA

NORTHERN MARIANA ISLANDS (U.S.)

MARIANA ISLANDS

GUAM (U.S.)

Koror

PALAU ISLANDS

PALAU

FEDERATED STATES OF MICRONES

CAROLINE ISLANDS

Equator

NEW GUINEA

PAPUA NEW GUINEA

NEW BRITAIN

BOUGAINVILL

Mt. Giluwe 14,330 Ft.

Port Moresby

Honiara

ARAFURA SEA

Cape York

CAPE YORK PENINSULA

CORAL SEA

Darwin

Cape Londonderry

Gulf of Carpentaria

Cooktown

Cairns

Cape Leveque

Normanton

Townsville

INDIAN OCEAN

GREAT DIVIDING RANGE

Cape Capricorn

Sandy Cape

GREAT SANDY DESERT

Alice Springs

AUSTRALIA

Brisbane

North West Cape

△ Ayers Rock 2,844 Ft.

Tropic of Capricorn

Carnarvon

Carnegie

GREAT VICTORIA DESERT

Darling

GREAT DIVIDING RANGE

Newcas

Sydney

Kalgoorlie-Boulder

Port Augusta

Adelaide

Mt. Kosciuszko 7,313 Ft.

Canberra

Wanneroo

Perth

Great Australian Bight

Cape Arid

Cape Carnot

Cape Jaffa

Melbourne

Cape Howe

Cape Naturaliste

Hood Point

Cape Otway

Cape Grim

Cape Portla

Point D'Entrecasteaux

TASMANIA

Hobart

Mt. Osse 5,305 Ft.

South East

Snowcapped Aoraki, or Mount Cook, is New Zealand's highest mountain.

The starfish plays an important role in Oceania's reef systems.

10   11   12   13   14   15   16   17″

New Zealand, called "Aoteraroa" or "long white cloud" by its original Maori inhabitants, is the second-largest country in Oceania (after Australia). Most people live on North Island in Auckland and Wellington. While South Island is known for its mountains and deep fjords, North Island has its share of wonders: Glowworms light deep cave chambers, while hot springs and geysers provide geothermal power and heat for the island's inhabitants. New Zealand has far more sheep than people, and wool and mutton are two of its leading exports.

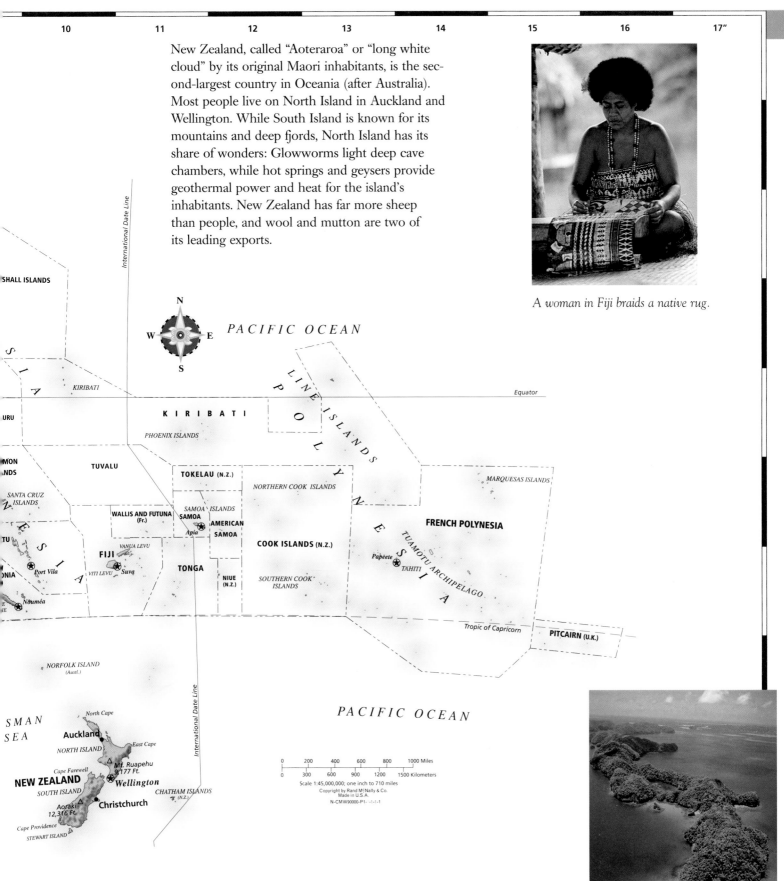

A woman in Fiji braids a native rug.

International Date Line

N
W · E
S

PACIFIC OCEAN

SHALL ISLANDS

S
I
A

KIRIBATI

Equator

K I R I B A T I

L
I
N
E

I
S
L
A
N
D
S

PHOENIX ISLANDS

URU

MON
NDS

TUVALU

TOKELAU (N.Z.)

NORTHERN COOK ISLANDS

MARQUESAS ISLANDS

*SANTA CRUZ
ISLANDS*

Z
E

SAMOA ISLANDS

**WALLIS AND FUTUNA
(Fr.)**

SAMOA

Apia

**AMERICAN
SAMOA**

FRENCH POLYNESIA

TU

VANUA LEVU

COOK ISLANDS (N.Z.)

P
O
L
Y
N
E

T
U
A
M
O
T
U

A
R
C
H
I
P
E
L
A
G
O

Papeete

ONIA

Port Vila

FIJI

VITI LEVU   *Suva*

TONGA

**NIUE
(N.Z.)**

*SOUTHERN COOK
ISLANDS*

S
I
A

TAHITI

IE

Nouméa

Tropic of Capricorn

PITCAIRN (U.K.)

*NORFOLK ISLAND
(Austl.)*

International Date Line

PACIFIC OCEAN

S M A N
S E A

North Cape

Auckland

NORTH ISLAND

East Cape

△ *Mt. Ruapehu
9,177 Ft.*

NEW ZEALAND

Cape Farewell

Wellington

SOUTH ISLAND

*CHATHAM ISLANDS
(N.Z.)*

*Aoraki
12,316 Ft.*

△

Christchurch

Cape Providence

STEWART ISLAND

0   200   400   600   800   1000 Miles
0   300   600   900   1200   1500 Kilometers
Scale 1:45,000,000; one inch to 710 miles
Copyright by Rand McNally & Co.
Made in U.S.A.
N-CMW90000-P1- -:-:-1

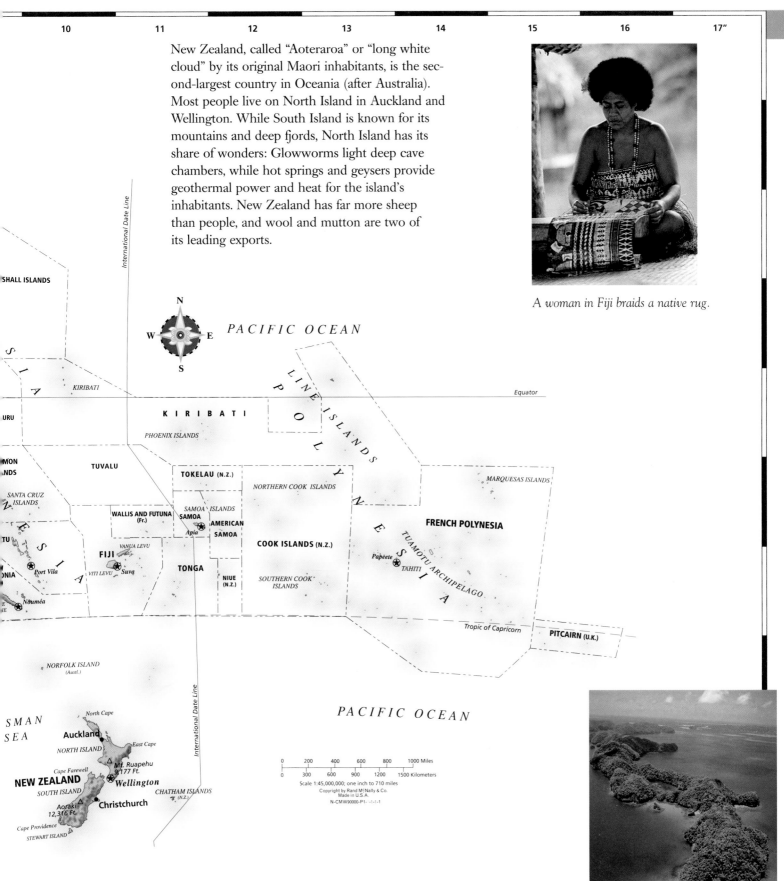

*Reefs dominate the volcanic
island of Palau.*

ANTARCTICA

Antarctica is the coldest, driest, and windiest place on Earth. The continent lies directly over the South Pole, and its rocky land is almost entirely covered by a layer of ice that averages 6,500 feet (2,000 meters) thick. Were the ice to melt, the water would be enough to submerge th Alps. The Transantarctic Mountains divide the continent into East and West Antarctica. In East Antarctica, where the South Pole is located, the ice sheet covers bedrock. West Antarctica is a series of islands connected–and in some cases covered–by dense ice. More than ninety percent of Earth's glacial ice is located in Antarctica. In the winter, the ice sheet extends far into the ocean, doubling the continent's size. Despite all this frozen water, Antarctica's average precipitation of around two inches (50 millimeters) per year makes it one of Earth's largest deserts.

Antarctica Facts

Area: 5,400,000 square miles (14,000,000 square kilometers)

Highest Mountain: Vinson Massif, 16,066 feet (4,897 meters)

Lowest Point: Deep Lake, -184 feet (-56 meters)

Coldest Spot: Vostok, July 21, 1983, -129° Fahrenheit (-89° Celsius)

Very little plant life can survive in such cold conditions, but certain lichens, molds, mosses, fungi, algae, and bacteria live in this arctic habitat.

Antarctica has no permanent residents. Instead, groups of researchers from all over the world come to visit scientific stations and to learn more about this forbidding, fascinating continent.

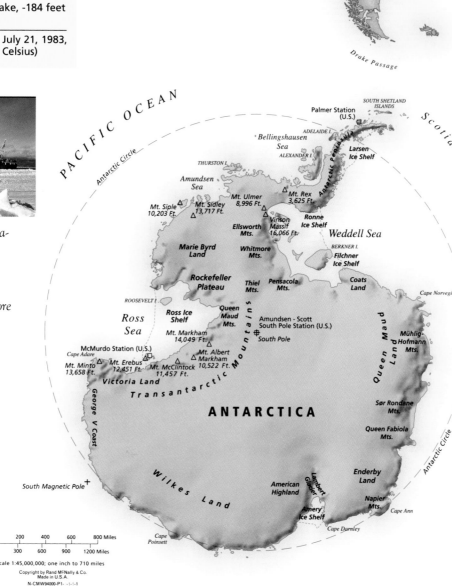

Drake Passage

PACIFIC OCEAN

Antarctic Circle

SOUTH SHETLAND ISLANDS

Palmer Station (U.S.)

ADELAIDE I.

Bellingshausen Sea

Scotia Sea

ALEXANDER I.

Larsen Ice Shelf

Antarctic Peninsula

THURSTON I.

Amundsen Sea

Mt. Ulmer 8,996 Ft.

Mt. Rex 3,625 Ft.

Mt. Siple 10,203 Ft.

Mt. Sidley 13,717 Ft.

Vinson Massif 16,066 Ft.

Ronne Ice Shelf

Ellsworth Mts.

Weddell Sea

Marie Byrd Land

Whitmore Mts.

BERKNER I.

Filchner Ice Shelf

Rockefeller Plateau

Thiel Mts.

Pensacola Mts.

Coats Land

Cape Norvegia

ROOSEVELT I.

Ross Ice Shelf

Queen Maud Mts.

Amundsen - Scott South Pole Station (U.S.)

South Pole

Queen Maud Land

Mühlig-Hofmann Mts.

Ross Sea

Mt. Markham 14,049 Ft.

McMurdo Station (U.S.)

Cape Adare

Mt. Albert Markham 10,522 Ft.

Mt. Erebus 12,451 Ft.

Mt. McClintock 11,457 Ft.

Transantarctic Mountains

Sør Rondane Mts.

Mt. Minto 13,658 Ft.

Victoria Land

Queen Fabiola Mts.

ANTARCTICA

George V Coast

South Magnetic Pole +

Wilkes Land

American Highland

Lambert Glacier

Enderby Land

Napier Mts.

Antarctic Circle

Cape Ann

Amery Ice Shelf

Cape Poinsett

Cape Darnley

ATLANTIC OCEAN

0 200 400 600 800 Miles
0 300 600 900 1200 Miles

Scale 1:45,000,000; one inch to 710 miles

Copyright by Rand McNally & Co.
Made in U.S.A.
N-CMW94000-P1- -:-:-1

INDIAN OCEAN

Seabirds flock to Antarctica to roost, and several different species of penguin (above left) live on the ice, near the coast (left). No land mammals live here, but an abundance of krill—tiny shrimplike creatures—provides food for a large population of aquatic mammals, including a variety of whales (below) and seals.

Country Flag and Fact File

North America

Anguilla (U.K.)
Area: 35 sq mi (91 sq km)
Population: 11,000
Capital: The Valley

Antigua and Barbuda
Area: 171 sq mi (442 sq km)
Population: 64,000
Capital: St. John's

Bahamas
Area: 5,382 sq mi
  (13,939 sq km)
Population: 282,000
Capital: Nassau

Barbados
Area: 166 sq mi (430 sq km)
Population: 259,000
Capital: Bridgetown

Belize
Area: 8,866 sq mi
  (22,963 sq km)
Population: 233,000
Capital: Belmopan

Canada
Area: 3,849,674 sq mi
(9,970,610 sq km)
Population: 30,450,000
Capital: Ottawa

Costa Rica
Area: 19,730 sq mi
  (51,100 sq km)
Population: 3,639,000
Capital: San José

Cuba
Area: 42,804 sq mi
  (110,861 sq km)
Population: 11,075,000
Capital: Havana

Dominica
Area: 305 sq mi (790 sq km)
Population: 66,000
Capital: Roseau

Dominican Republic
Area: 18,704 sq mi
  (48,442 sq km)
Population: 8,064,000
Capital: Santo Domingo

El Salvador
Area: 8,124 sq mi
  (21,041 sq km)
Population: 5,797,000
Capital: San Salvador

Greenland (Denmark)
Area: 840,004 sq mi
  (2,175,600 sq km)
Population: 59,000
Capital: Godthåb

Grenada
Area: 133 sq mi (344 sq km)
Population: 96,000
Capital: St. George's

Guatemala
Area: 42,042 sq mi
  (108,889 sq km)
Population: 12,170,000
Capital: Guatemala

Haiti
Area: 10,714 sq mi
  (27,750 sq km)
Population: 6,833,000
Capital: Port-au-Prince

Honduras
Area: 43,277 sq mi
  (112,088 sq km)
Population: 5,931,000
Capital: Tegucigalpa

Jamaica
Area: 4,244 sq mi
  (10,991 sq km)
Population: 2,644,000
Capital: Kingston

Mexico
Area: 759,533 sq mi
  (1,967,183 sq km)
Population: 99,430,000
Capital: Mexico City

Nicaragua
Area: 50,054 sq mi
  (129,640 sq km)
Population: 4,650,000
Capital: Managua

Panama
Area: 29,157 sq mi
  (75,517 sq km)
Population: 2,757,000
Capital: Panamá

Puerto Rico (U.S.)
Area: 3,515 sq mi
  (9,104 sq km)
Population: 3,870,000
Capital: San Juan

St. Kitts and Nevis
Area: 104 sq mi (269 sq km)
Population: 42,000
Capital: Basseterre

St. Lucia
Area: 238 sq mi (616 sq km)
Population: 153,000
Capital: Castries

St. Vincent and the Grenadines
Area: 150 sq mi (388 sq km)
Population: 120,000
Capital: Kingstown

Trinidad and Tobago
Area: 1,980 sq mi
  (5,128 sq km)
Population: 1,110,000
Capital: Port of Spain

United States
Area: 3,787,425 sq mi
  (9,809,431 sq km)
Population: 271,490,000
Capital: Washington

South America

Argentina
Area: 1,073,519 sq mi
(2,780,400 sq km)
Population: 36,500,000
Capitals: Buenos Aires (de facto) and Viedma (future)

Bolivia
Area: 424,165 sq mi
(1,098,581 sq km)
Population: 7,904,000
Capitals: La Paz (seat of government) and Sucre (legal capital)

Brazil
Area: 3,300,172 sq mi
(8,547,404 sq km)
Population: 170,860,000
Capital: Brasília

Chile
Area: 292,135 sq mi
(756,626 sq km)
Population: 14,880,000
Capital: Santiago

Colombia
Area: 440,831 sq mi
(1,141,748 sq km)
Population: 38,950,000
Capital: Bogotá

Ecuador
Area: 105,037 sq mi
(272,045 sq km)
Population: 12,450,000
Capital: Quito

Guyana
Area: 83,000 sq mi
(214,969 sq km)
Population: 706,000
Capital: Georgetown

Paraguay
Area: 157,048 sq mi
(406,752 sq km)
Population: 5,362,000
Capital: Asunción

Peru
Area: 496,225 sq mi
(1,285,216 sq km)
Population: 26,365,000
Capital: Lima

Suriname
Area: 63,251 sq mi
(163,820 sq km)
Population: 430,000
Capital: Paramaribo

Uruguay
Area: 68,500 sq mi
(177,414 sq km)
Population: 3,297,000
Capital: Montevideo

Venezuela
Area: 352,144 sq mi
(912,050 sq km)
Population: 23,005,000
Capital: Caracas

Europe

Albania
Area: 11,100 sq mi
(28,748 sq km)
Population: 3,347,000
Capital: Tiranë

Andorra
Area: 175 sq mi
(453 sq km)
Population: 65,000
Capital: Andorra

Austria
Area: 32,377 sq mi
(83,856 sq km)
Population: 8,136,000
Capital: Vienna

Belarus
Area: 80,155 sq mi
(207,600 sq km)
Population: 10,405,000
Capital: Minsk

Belgium
Area: 11,783 sq mi
(30,518 sq km)
Population: 10,180,000
Capital: Brussels

Bosnia and Herzegovina
Area: 19,741 sq mi
(51,129 sq km)
Population: 3,427,000
Capital: Sarajevo

Bulgaria
Area: 42,855 sq mi
(110,994 sq km)
Population: 8,215,000
Capital: Sofia

Croatia
Area: 21,829 sq mi
(56,538 sq km)
Population: 4,675,000
Capital: Zagreb

Czech Republic
Area: 30,450 sq mi
(78,864 sq km)
Population: 10,280,000
Capital: Prague

Denmark
Area: 16,639 sq mi
(43,094 sq km)
Population: 5,347,000
Capital: Copenhagen

Estonia
Area: 17,413 sq mi
(45,100 sq km)
Population: 1,414,000
Capital: Tallinn

Finland
Area: 130,559 sq mi
(338,145 sq km)
Population: 5,154,000
Capital: Helsinki

France
Area: 211,208 sq mi
(547,026 sq km)
Population: 58,890,000
Capital: Paris

Germany
Area: 137,822 sq mi
(356,955 sq km)
Population: 82,700,000
Capital: Berlin

Greece
Area: 50,949 sq mi
 (131,957 sq km)
Population: 10,685,000
Capital: Athens

Lithuania
Area: 25,213 sq mi
 (65,300 sq km)
Population: 3,592,000
Capital: Vilnius

Norway
Area: 149,405 sq mi
 (386,958 sq km)
Population: 4,430,000
Capital: Oslo

Spain
Area: 194,885 sq mi
 (504,750 sq km)
Population: 39,150,000
Capital: Madrid

Hungary
Area: 35,919 sq mi
 (93,030 sq km)
Population: 10,195,000
Capital: Budapest

Luxembourg
Area: 999 sq mi
 (2,586 sq km)
Population: 427,000
Capital: Luxembourg

Poland
Area: 121,196 sq mi
 (313,895 sq km)
Population: 38,600,000
Capital: Warsaw

Sweden
Area: 173,732 sq mi
 (449,964 sq km)
Population: 8,899,000
Capital: Stockholm

Iceland
Area: 39,769 sq mi
 (103,000 sq km)
Population: 272,000
Capital: Reykjavík

Macedonia
Area: 9,928 sq mi
 (25,713 sq km)
Population: 2,016,000
Capital: Skopje

Portugal
Area: 35,516 sq mi
 (91,985 sq km)
Population: 9,925,000
Capital: Lisbon

Switzerland
Area: 15,943 sq mi
 (41,293 sq km)
Population: 7,268,000
Capital: Bern

Ireland
Area: 27,137 sq mi
 (70,285 sq km)
Population: 3,626,000
Capital: Dublin

Malta
Area: 122 sq mi (316 sq km)
Population: 381,000
Capital: Valletta

Romania
Area: 91,699 sq mi
 (237,500 sq km)
Population: 22,360,000
Capital: Bucharest

Ukraine
Area: 233,090 sq mi
 (603,700 sq km)
Population: 49,965,000
Capital: Kiev

Italy
Area: 116,336 sq mi
 (301,309 sq km)
Population: 56,760,000
Capital: Rome

Moldova
Area: 13,012 sq mi
 (33,700 sq km)
Population: 4,459,000
Capital: Chişinău

San Marino
Area: 24 sq mi (61 sq km)
Population: 25,000
Capital: San Marino

United Kingdom
Area: 94,249 sq mi
 (244,101 sq km)
Population: 59,040,000
Capital: London

Latvia
Area: 24,595 sq mi
 (63,700 sq km)
Population: 2,368,000
Capital: Rīga

Monaco
Area: 0.8 sq mi (2 sq km)
Population: 32,000
Capital: Monaco

Slovakia
Area: 18,933 sq mi
 (49,035 sq km)
Population: 5,395,000
Capital: Bratislava

Vatican City
Area: 0.2 sq mi (0.4 sq km)
Population: 1,000
Capital: Vatican City

Liechtenstein
Area: 62 sq mi (160 sq km)
Population: 32,000
Capital: Vaduz

Netherlands
Area: 16,164 sq mi
 (41,864 sq km)
Population: 15,770,000
Capitals: Amsterdam
 (designated) and The Hague
 (seat of government)

Slovenia
Area: 7,820 sq mi
 (20,253 sq km)
Population: 1,971,000
Capital: Ljubljana

Yugoslavia
Area: 39,449 sq mi
 (102,173 sq km)
Population: 11,205,000
Capital: Belgrade

Africa

Algeria
Area: 919,595 sq mi
(2,381,741 sq km)
Population: 30,805,000
Capital: Algiers

Angola
Area: 481,354 sq mi
(1,246,700 sq km)
Population: 11,020,000
Capital: Luanda

Benin
Area: 43,475 sq mi
(112,600 sq km)
Population: 6,202,000
Capitals: Porto-Novo
(designated) and Cotonou
(de facto)

Botswana
Area: 224,711 sq mi
(582,000 sq km)
Population: 1,456,000
Capital: Gaborone

Burkina Faso
Area: 105,869 sq mi
(274,200 sq km)
Population: 11,420,000
Capital: Ouagadougou

Burundi
Area: 10,745 sq mi
(27,830 sq km)
Population: 5,634,000
Capital: Bujumbura

Cameroon
Area: 183,568 sq mi
(475,440 sq km)
Population: 15,240,000
Capital: Yaoundé

Cape Verde
Area: 1,557 sq mi
(4,033 sq km)
Population: 403,000
Capital: Praia

Central African Republic
Area: 240,535 sq mi
(622,984 sq km)
Population: 3,410,000
Capital: Bangui

Chad
Area: 495,755 sq mi
(1,284,000 sq km)
Population: 7,458,000
Capital: N'Djamena

Comoros
Area: 863 sq mi
(2,235 sq km)
Population: 554,000
Capital: Moroni

Congo
Area: 132,047 sq mi
(342,000 sq km)
Population: 2,688,000
Capital: Brazzaville

Cote d'Ivoire
Area: 124,518 sq mi
(322,500 sq km)
Population: 15,630,000
Capitals: Abidjan (de facto)
and Yamoussoukro (future)

Dem. Rep. of the Congo
Area: 905,446 sq mi
(2,345,095 sq km)
Population: 49,735,000
Capital: Kinshasa

Djibouti
Area: 8,958 sq mi
(23,200 sq km)
Population: 444,000
Capital: Djibouti

Egypt
Area: 386,662 sq mi
(1,001,449 sq km)
Population: 66,660,000
Capital: Cairo

Equatorial Guinea
Area: 10,831 sq mi
(28,051 sq km)
Population: 460,000
Capital: Malabo

Eritrea
Area: 36,170 sq mi
(93,679 sq km)
Population: 3,907,000
Capital: Asmera

Ethiopia
Area: 446,953 sq mi
(1,157,603 sq km)
Population: 59,040,000
Capital: Addis Ababa

Gabon
Area: 103,347 sq mi
(267,667 sq km)
Population: 1,217,000
Capital: Libreville

The Gambia
Area: 4,127 sq mi
(10,689 sq km)
Population: 1,314,000
Capital: Banjul

Ghana
Area: 92,098 sq mi
(238,533 sq km)
Population: 18,695,000
Capital: Accra

Guinea
Area: 94,926 sq mi
(245,857 sq km)
Population: 7,508,000
Capital: Conakry

Guinea-Bissau
Area: 13,948 sq mi
(36,125 sq km)
Population: 1,220,000
Capital: Bissau

Kenya
Area: 224,961 sq mi
(582,646 sq km)
Population: 28,580,000
Capital: Nairobi

Lesotho
Area: 11,720 sq mi
(30,355 sq km)
Population: 2,110,000
Capital: Maseru

Liberia
Area: 38,250 sq mi
(99,067 sq km)
Population: 2,852,000
Capital: Monrovia

Libya
Area: 679,362 sq mi
 (1,759,540 sq km)
Population: 4,934,000
Capital: Tripoli

Madagascar
Area: 226,658 sq mi
 (587,041 sq km)
Population: 14,665,000
Capital: Antananarivo

Malawi
Area: 45,747 sq mi
 (118,484 sq km)
Population: 9,922,000
Capital: Lilongwe

Mali
Area: 482,077 sq mi
 (1,248,574 sq km)
Population: 10,275,000
Capital: Bamako

Mauritania
Area: 397,955 sq mi
 (1,030,700 sq km)
Population: 2,543,000
Capital: Nouakchott

Mauritius
Area: 788 sq mi (2,040 sq km)
Population: 1,175,000
Capital: Port Louis

Morocco
Area: 172,414 sq mi
 (446,550 sq km)
Population: 29,390,000
Capital: Rabat

Mozambique
Area: 308,642 sq mi
 (799,380 sq km)
Population: 19,895,000
Capital: Maputo

Namibia
Area: 317,818 sq mi
 (823,144 sq km)
Population: 1,635,000
Capital: Windhoek

Niger
Area: 489,191 sq mi
 (1,267,000 sq km)
Population: 9,815,000
Capital: Niamey

Nigeria
Area: 356,669 sq mi
 (923,768 sq km)
Population: 112,170,000
Capital: Abuja

Rwanda
Area: 10,169 sq mi
 (26,338 sq km)
Population: 8,055,000
Capital: Kigali

Sao Tome and Principe
Area: 372 sq mi (964 sq km)
Population: 152,000
Capital: São Tomé

Senegal
Area: 75,951 sq mi
 (196,712 sq km)
Population: 9,885,000
Capital: Dakar

Seychelles
Area: 175 sq mi (453 sq km)
Population: 79,000
Capital: Victoria

Sierra Leone
Area: 27,925 sq mi
 (72,325 sq km)
Population: 5,182,000
Capital: Freetown

Somalia
Area: 246,201 sq mi
 (637,657 sq km)
Population: 6,993,000
Capital: Mogadishu

South Africa
Area: 471,009 sq mi
 (1,219,909 sq km)
Population: 43,140,000
Capitals: Pretoria
 (administrative), Cape
 Town (legislative), and
 Bloemfontein (judicial)

Sudan
Area: 967,499 sq mi
 (2,505,813 sq km)
Population: 34,010,000
Capital: Khartoum

Swaziland
Area: 6,704 sq mi
 (17,364 sq km)
Population: 975,000
Capitals: Mbabane
 (administrative) and
 Lobamba (legislative)

Tanzania
Area: 364,900 sq mi
 (945,087 sq km)
Population: 30,935,000
Capitals: Dar es Salaam
 (de facto) and Dodoma
 (legislative)

Togo
Area: 21,925 sq mi
 (56,785 sq km)
Population: 4,992,000
Capital: Lomé

Tunisia
Area: 63,170 sq mi
 (163,610 sq km)
Population: 9,448,000
Capital: Tunis

Uganda
Area: 93,104 sq mi
 (241,139 sq km)
Population: 22,485,000
Capital: Kampala

Zambia
Area: 290,586 sq mi
 (752,614 sq km)
Population: 9,561,000
Capital: Lusaka

Zimbabwe
Area: 150,873 sq mi
 (390,759 sq km)
Population: 11,105,000
Capital: Harare

Asia

Afghanistan
Area: 251,826 sq mi
(652,225 sq km)
Population: 25,315,000
Capital: Kabul

Armenia
Area: 11,506 sq mi
(29,800 sq km)
Population: 3,416,000
Capital: Yerevan

Azerbaijan
Area: 33,436 sq mi
(86,600 sq km)
Population: 7,883,000
Capital: Baku

Bahrain
Area: 267 sq mi (691 sq km)
Population: 622,000
Capital: Al Manāmah

Bangladesh
Area: 55,598 sq mi
(143,998 sq km)
Population: 126,110,000
Capital: Dhaka

Bhutan
Area: 17,954 sq mi
(46,500 sq km)
Population: 1,930,000
Capital: Thimphu

Brunei
Area: 2,226 sq mi
(5,765 sq km)
Population: 319,000
Capital: Bandar Seri Begawan

Cambodia
Area: 69,898 sq mi
(181,035 sq km)
Population: 11,485,000
Capital: Phnum Pénh

China
Area: 3,690,045 sq mi
(9,557,172 sq km)
Population: 1,242,070,000
Capital: Beijing

Cyprus
Area: 2,277 sq mi
(5,896 sq km)
Population: 615,000
Capital: Nicosia

Georgia
Area: 26,911 sq mi
(69,700 sq km)
Population: 5,085,000
Capital: Tbilisi

India
Area: 1,237,061 sq mi
(3,203,975 sq km)
Population: 992,470,000
Capital: New Delhi

Indonesia
Area: 752,409 sq mi
(1,948,732 sq km)
Population: 214,530,000
Capital: Jakarta

Iran
Area: 630,578 sq mi
(1,633,189 sq km)
Population: 64,830,000
Capital: Tehrān

Iraq
Area: 169,235 sq mi
(438,317 sq km)
Population: 22,070,000
Capital: Baghdād

Israel
Area: 8,019 sq mi
(20,770 sq km)
Population: 5,353,000
Capital: Jerusalem

Japan
Area: 145,850 sq mi
(377,750 sq km)
Population: 126,060,000
Capital: Tōkyō

Jordan
Area: 35,135 sq mi
(91,000 sq km)
Population: 4,491,000
Capital: 'Ammān

Kazakhstan
Area: 1,049,155 sq mi
(2,717,300 sq km)
Population: 16,835,000
Capital: Astana

Kuwait
Area: 6,880 sq mi
(17,818 sq km)
Population: 1,952,000
Capital: Kuwait

Kyrgyzstan
Area: 76,641 sq mi
(198,500 sq km)
Population: 4,531,000
Capital: Bishkek

Laos
Area: 91,429 sq mi
(236,800 sq km)
Population: 5,334,000
Capital: Viangchan

Lebanon
Area: 4,016 sq mi
(10,400 sq km)
Population: 3,534,000
Capital: Beirut

Malaysia
Area: 127,320 sq mi
(329,758 sq km)
Population: 21,155,000
Capital: Kuala Lumpur

Maldives
Area: 115 sq mi (298 sq km)
Population: 295,000
Capital: Male'

Mongolia
Area: 604,829 sq mi
(1,566,500 sq km)
Population: 2,599,000
Capital: Ulan Bator

Myanmar
Area: 261,228 sq mi
(676,578 sq km)
Population: 47,700,000
Capital: Yangon

Nepal
Area: 56,827 sq mi
  (147,181 sq km)
Population: 23,995,000
Capital: Kathmandu

North Cyprus
Area: 1,295 sq mi
  (3,355 sq km)
Population: 137,000
Capital: Nicosia

North Korea
Area: 46,540 sq mi
  (120,538 sq km)
Population: 21,230,000
Capital: P'yŏngyang

Oman
Area: 82,030 sq mi
  (212,457 sq km)
Population: 2,405,000
Capital: Muscat

Pakistan
Area: 339,732 sq mi
  (879,902 sq km)
Population: 136,620,000
Capital: Islāmābād

Philippines
Area: 115,831 sq mi
  (300,000 sq km)
Population: 78,530,000
Capital: Manila

Qatar
Area: 4,412 sq mi
  (11,427 sq km)
Population: 710,000
Capital: Doha

Russia
Area: 6,592,849 sq mi
  (17,075,400 sq km)
Population: 146,630,000
Capital: Moscow

Saudi Arabia
Area: 830,000 sq mi
  (2,149,690 sq km)
Population: 21,140,000
Capital: Riyadh

Singapore
Area: 246 sq mi (636 sq km)
Population: 3,511,000
Capital: Singapore

South Korea
Area: 38,230 sq mi
  (99,016 sq km)
Population: 46,650,000
Capital: Seoul

Sri Lanka
Area: 24,962 sq mi
  (64,652 sq km)
Population: 19,040,000
Capitals: Colombo
  (designated) and
  Sri Jayawardenepura
  (seat of government)

Syria
Area: 71,498 sq mi
  (185,180 sq km)
Population: 16,955,000
Capital: Damascus

Taiwan
Area: 13,900 sq mi
  (36,002 sq km)
Population: 22,010,000
Capital: T'aipei

Tajikistan
Area: 55,251 sq mi
  (143,100 sq km)
Population: 6,059,000
Capital: Dushanbe

Thailand
Area: 198,115 sq mi
  (513,115 sq km)
Population: 60,330,000
Capital: Bangkok

Turkey
Area: 300,948 sq mi
  (779,452 sq km)
Population: 65,090,000
Capital: Ankara

Turkmenistan
Area: 188,456 sq mi
  (488,100 sq km)
Population: 4,332,000
Capital: Ashgabat

United Arab Emirates
Area: 32,278 sq mi
  (83,600 sq km)
Population: 2,323,000
Capital: Abu Dhabi

Uzbekistan
Area: 172,742 sq mi
  (447,400 sq km)
Population: 23,940,000
Capital: Tashkent

Vietnam
Area: 127,428 sq mi
  (330,036 sq km)
Population: 76,790,000
Capital: Hanoi

Yemen
Area: 203,850 sq mi
  (527,968 sq km)
Population: 16,660,000
Capital: Sanaa

Australia and Oceania

Australia
Area: 2,966,155 sq mi
  (7,682,300 sq km)
Population: 18,735,000
Capital: Canberra

Cook Islands (New Zealand)
Area: 91 sq mi (236 sq km)
Population: 20,000
Capital: Avarua

Fiji
Area: 7,056 sq mi
  (18,274 sq km)
Population: 808,000
Capital: Suva

Kiribati
Area: 313 sq mi (811 sq km)
Population: 85,000
Capital: Bairiki

Marshall Islands
Area: 70 sq mi (181 sq km)
Population: 64,000
Capital: Majuro (island)

Federated States of Micronesia
Area: 271 sq mi (702 sq km)
Population: 132,000
Capital: Palikir

Nauru
Area: 8.1 sq mi (21 sq km)
Population: 11,000
Capital: Yaren District

New Zealand
Area: 104,454 sq mi
  (270,534 sq km)
Population: 3,644,000
Capital: Wellington

Niue (New Zealand)
Area: 100 sq mi (259 sq km)
Population: 1,600
Capital: Alofi

Northern Mariana Islands (U.S.)
Area: 184 sq mi (477 sq km)
Population: 68,000
Capital: Saipan (island)

Palau
Area: 196 sq mi (508 sq km)
Population: 18,000
Capitals: Koror (de facto)
  and Melekeok (future)

Papua New Guinea
Area: 178,703 sq mi
  (462,840 sq km)
Population: 4,652,000
Capital: Port Moresby

Samoa
Area: 1,093 sq mi
  (2,831 sq km)
Population: 228,000
Capital: Apia

Solomon Islands
Area: 10,954 sq mi
  (28,370 sq km)
Population: 448,000
Capital: Honaira

Tonga
Area: 288 sq mi
  (747 sq km)
Population: 108,000
Capital: Nuku'alofa

Tuvalu
Area: 10 sq mi (26 sq km)
Population: 10,000
Capital: Funafuti

Vanuatu
Area: 4,707 sq mi
  (12,190 sq km)
Population: 187,000
Capital: Port Vila

Territories and Dependencies

North America

Country Name	Area	Population	Capital
Aruba (Netherlands)	75 sq mi (193 sq km)	68,000	Oranjestad
Bermuda (U.K.)	21 sq mi (54 sq km)	62,000	Hamilton
British Virgin Islands (U.K.)	59 sq mi (153 sq km)	19,000	Road Town
Cayman Islands (U.K.)	100 sq mi (259 sq km)	39,000	George Town
Guadeloupe (France)	657 sq mi (1,702 sq km)	418,000	Basse-Terre
Martinique (France)	436 sq mi (1,128 sq km)	409,000	Fort-de-France
Montserrat (U.K.)	39 sq mi (102 sq km)	13,000	Plymouth
Netherlands Antilles (Netherlands)	309 sq mi (800 sq km)	207,000	Willemstad
St. Pierre and Miquelon (France)	93 sq mi (242 sq km)	7,000	Saint-Pierre
Turks and Caicos Islands (U.K.)	193 sq mi (500 sq km)	16,000	Grand Turk
Virgin Islands (U.S.)	133 sq mi (344 sq km)	119,000	Charlotte Amalie

South America

Falkland Islands (U.K.)	4,700 sq mi (12,173 sq km)	2,900	Stanley
French Guiana (France)	32,253 sq mi (83,534 sq km)	166,000	Cayenne
South Georgia and the South Sandwich Islands (U.K.)	1,450 sq mi (3,755 sq km)	none	none

Europe

Faroe Islands (Denmark)	540 sq mi (1,399 sq km)	42,000	Tórshavn
Gibraltar (U.K.)	2.3 sq mi (6.0 sq km)	29,000	Gibraltar
Guernsey (U.K.)	30 sq mi (78 sq km)	65,000	St. Peter Port
Isle of Man (U.K.)	221 sq mi (572 sq km)	75,000	Douglas
Jersey (U.K.)	45 sq mi (116 sq km)	89,000	St. Helier

Africa

British Indian Ocean Territory (U.K.)	23 sq mi (60 sq km)	none	none
Mayotte (France)	144 sq mi (374 sq km)	146,000	Mamoudzou
Reunion (France)	967 sq mi (2,504 sq km)	711,000	Saint-Denis
St. Helena (U.K.)	121 sq mi (314 sq km)	7,000	Jamestown
Spanish North Africa (Spain)	12 sq mi (32 sq km)	153,000	none

Australia and Oceania

American Samoa (U.S.)	77 sq mi (199 sq km)	63,000	Pago Pago
Christmas Island (Australia)	52 sq mi (135 sq km)	2,300	Settlement
Cocos Islands (Australia)	5.4 sq mi (14 sq km)	600	West Island
French Polynesia (France)	1,360 sq mi (3,521 sq km)	228,000	Papeete
Guam (U.S.)	209 sq mi (541 sq km)	150,000	Agana
Johnson Atoll (U.S.)	0.5 sq mi (1.3 sq km)	1,100	none
Midway Islands (U.S.)	2 sq mi (5.2 sq km)	140	none
New Caledonia (France)	7,172 sq mi (18,575 sq km)	196,000	Nouméa
Norfolk Island (France)	14 sq mi (36 sq km)	2,200	Kingston
Pitcairn (U.K.)	19 sq mi (49 sq km)	400	Adamstown
Tokelau (New Zealand)	4.6 sq mi (12 sq km)	1,400	none
Wake Island (U.S.)	3 sq mi (7.8 sq km)	200	none
Wallis and Futuna (France)	99 sq mi (255 sq km)	15,000	Mata-Utu

Glossary

A

agriculture Land use for the growing of crops and the raising of livestock; farming.

arid Extremely dry; lacking moisture.

B

border The region or line around the edge of a country, state, province, or territory that separates it from another country, state, province, or territory.

C

cape An expanse of land, shaped like a point, extending into water.

capital A city that is the seat of a country or state government.

cartographer A person who makes maps.

cash crop Crops grown to sell commercially, often to foreign countries.

climate Weather patterns within a region that happen over long periods of time.

continent A major landmass surrounded by water. Earth has seven continents.

country A nation with its own distinct name, land area, government, language, and culture.

crop Vegetables, grains, cotton, or other plants grown by farmers.

culture Customs, traditions, and a way of life that people share.

D

desert An area of hot or cold land that is dry, with little or no rainfall.

E

economy The organization and management of a country's resources, industries, and services.

elevation The height of land above sea level, measured in feet or meters.

environment The natural conditions of an area that include climate, land, and resources.

equator The imaginary line of 0° latitude that circles Earth at its center.

ethnic group People who share traits, such as language, culture, heritage, and lifestyle.

export To send or sell goods to other countries.

F

fertile Land with rich soil that is suitable for growing crops.

fjord A deep, narrow inlet of the sea bordered by steep cliffs; usually created by a glacier.

G

glacier A huge mass of slow-moving ice.

gulf A large bay; an area of a sea or ocean partly enclosed by land.

H

hemisphere A half of Earth that is divided East and West or North and South.

hydroelectric power The use of falling water to produce energy in the form of electricity.

I

iceberg A large, floating ice block that has broken off of a glacier or ice sheet.

import To bring goods in from a foreign country to use or sell.

L

latitude Imaginary horizontal lines measuring distance in degrees north or south of the equator.

longitude Imaginary vertical lines measuring distance in degrees east or west of the prime meridian.

M

mineral Naturally occurring substances within the earth, such as coal, copper, or iron ore.

N

nomads People who move from place to place in search of food, water, and pastures for themselves and animal herds.

O

ocean A huge body of salt water. Oceans cover nearly two-thirds of Earth's surface.

P

peninsula A narrow area of land surrounded on three sides by water.

permafrost Ground that is permanently frozen.

plain An area of land that is low and flat.

population The total number of people living in a region.

prime meridian The imaginary vertical line of 0° that runs through Greenwich, England from the North Pole to the South Pole.

R

rain forest Dense, tropical forest with abundant rainfall and humidity.

resources Substances occuring naturally that have value, such as water and minerals.

rural Having to do with the countryside; opposite of urban.

S

savanna A tree-scattered grassland.

scale The measure of distance on a map as it compares to actual distance.

subsistence farming Farming that produces enough food for farmers, their families, and perhaps a local market, but not enough to sell commercially.

swamp A wetland, or marsh.

T

temperate A mild climate that is neither hot nor cold.

trade The buying, selling, and exchanging of goods within or between countries.

tundra The cold, frozen plains of the Arctic regions.

U

urban Having to do with cities; opposite of rural.

V

volcano An opening in Earth's crust through which lava, steam, and ash erupt.

Index of Major Places on the Maps